James P. Thomas

The Military Challenges of Transatlantic Coalitions

Adelphi Paper 333

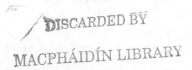

Oxford University Press, Great Clarendon Street, Oxford OX2 6DP
Oxford New York
Athens Auckland Bangkok Bombay Calcutta Cape Town
Dar es Salaam Delhi Florence Hong Kong Istanbul Karachi
Kuala Lumpur Madras Madrid Melbourne Mexico City
Nairobi Paris Singapore Taipei Tokyo Toronto
and associated companies in
Berlin Ibadan

Oxford is a trade mark of Oxford University Press

Published in the United States
by Oxford University Press Inc., New York

First published May 2000 by **Oxford University Press** for
The International Institute for Strategic Studies
Arundel House, 13–15 Arundel Street, Temple Place,
London WC2R 3DX, UK

Director John Chipman
Editor Mats R. Berdal
Assistant Editor Matthew Foley
Project Manager, Design and Production Mark Taylor

British Library Cataloguing in Publication Data
Data available

Library of Congress Cataloguing in Publication Data

ISBN 0-19-929005-9
ISSN 0567-932x

Contents

Glossary

ACTD	Advanced Concept Technology Demonstration (US)
ASM	air-to-surface missile
ATO	air tasking order
AWACS	airborne warning and control system
CAOC	Combined Air Operations Centre
CFAT	*Commandement de la Force d'Action Terrestre* (Land Action Force Command)
CJTF	Combined Joint Task Force (NATO)
COTs	commercial off-the-shelf technologies
CRONOS	Crisis Response Operations NATO Operating System
DCI	Defence Capabilities Initiative (NATO)
DRM	*Direction du Renseignement Militaire* (Directorate for Military Intelligence)
EMIA	*Etat-Major Interarmées de Planification Opérationnelle* (Joint Forces Planning Staff)
EU	European Union
FAR	*Force d'Action Rapide* (Rapid Reaction Force)
FOFA	Follow-On Forces Attack (NATO)
FüZBw	*Führungszentrum der Bundeswehr* (Joint Operational Command Centre)

GDP	gross domestic product
GBU	glide-bomb unit
GPS	global positioning system
HVK	*Hauptverteidigungskräfte* (Main Defence Forces)
IFF	Identification Friend or Foe
IFOR	Implementation Force (NATO)
JDAM	Joint Direct Attack Munition
JRRF	Joint Rapid Reaction Forces (UK)
JSTARS	Joint Surveillance Target Attack Radar System
JTIDS	Joint Tactical Information Distribution System
KFOR	Kosovo Force (NATO)
KRK	*Krisenreaktionskräfte* (Crisis Reaction Forces)
LOCE	Linked Operations/Intelligence Centres Europe
LPD	landing platform dock
MIDS	Multifunctional Information Distribution System
MTI	Moving Target Indicator
NBC	nuclear, biological and chemical
OSCE	Organisation for Security and Cooperation in Europe
PCIAT	*Poste de Commandement Interarmées de Théâtre* (Joint Theatre Command-and-Control Structure)
PJHQ	Permanent Joint Headquarters (UK)
QDR	Quadrennial Defense Review (US)
R&D	research and development
RAF	Royal Air Force (UK)
RMA	revolution in military affairs
SACEUR	Supreme Allied Commander Europe (NATO)
SACLANT	Supreme Allied Commander Atlantic (NATO)
SAM	surface-to-air missile
SDR	Strategic Defence Review (UK)
SEAD	suppression of enemy air defence
SFOR	Stabilisation Force (NATO)
SHAPE	Supreme Headquarters Allied Powers in Europe (NATO)

SIPRNET .... Secret Internet Protocol Network (US)

TACEVAL .... tactical evaluation (NATO)

TRI-TAC MSE .... Tri-Service Tactical Mobile Subscriber
Equipment (US)

UAV .... unmanned aerial vehicle

UNPROFOR .... UN Protection Force

Introduction

The US and its European Allies conducted more than 25 combined military operations between 1990 and 2000. These operations have informed the collective judgement of the transatlantic Allies that future Western military operations will normally be conducted within multinational coalitions.[1] The Allies depend upon coalitions, both to aggregate military power and to give political legitimacy to the use of force beyond their borders. Coalitions have accordingly become a defining characteristic of the modern Western style of war, and a political imperative for military action. However, this political imperative has not been matched by commensurate military preparations to ensure that coalitions are formed smoothly, and managed effectively. The growing discrepancy between the capabilities and concepts of the US and those of its European Allies has made balanced contributions impossible, and the coordination of forces difficult. Above all, peacetime consultation and pre-planning have been inadequate.

The transatlantic coalitions of the 1990s capitalised on the military relationship forged through the Atlantic Alliance during the Cold War. However, achieving an operationally effective coalition today poses three new challenges. First, to sustain international and domestic political support, modern coalitions must be much more discriminate in their use of force so as to minimise Allied, civilian and even enemy military casualties. This entails more specialised, and often expensive, equipment; a greater emphasis on force protection; increased pre-crisis consultation about collateral damage and targeting policies; and the closer coordination of fire systems. Second, the expeditionary nature of modern coalition operations has increased the need for readily deployable, all-regular forces, as well as long-range transport and logistics. Forces must be dispatched over great distances, and sustained for prolonged periods, often in regions lacking adequate logistical support or a well-developed infrastructure. National logistics and transport plans must be coordinated to ensure that forces arrive smoothly in distant theatres, particularly where their peaceful entry cannot be guaranteed. Third, coalitions are becoming vastly more complex, both in terms of how they are formed, and how they operate. This demands more integrated communications, command and control systems. Whereas during the Cold War, Allied forces would have been integrated at the corps or air-force-wing level, today's coalitions often come together at brigade or air-squadron levels, placing a higher premium on interoperability. As military operations have become less linear, faster and more complex, the importance of orchestrating the movements of coalition forces has increased. Both individually and through NATO, the US and its European Allies have all struggled to adapt their military forces to these new demands, and have done so at different rates, and in different ways. There has been insufficient coordination between them regarding how they should collectively prepare to meet these new operational criteria.

For the foreseeable future, the US and the major European states – the UK, France and Germany – will, for both political and military reasons, remain one another's most important potential coalition partners; some combination of these countries will probably be at the core of any future Western coalition. The extent of their preparation for multinational operations will thus be key in determining whether the endeavour succeeds or fails, and at what cost in lives and resources. Uneven and disjointed national preparations may erode the political will of the US and its European Allies to use force together to protect common Western values and interests. The increasing incompatibility of their forces may make operational integration more difficult, causing political leaders to lose confidence in their prospects of success. In the eyes of an adversary, insufficient preparation also weakens the credibility of a coalition's power. It reveals differences in US and European capabilities and operational concepts, as well as disagreements over political aims and rules of engagement, both of which could be exploited by an opponent. While a coalition's success breeds cohesion and inspires public support, the prospect of defeat or of a protracted engagement may make a coalition less effective and cohesive.[2] The political will to enter, or remain committed to, multinational actions could be undermined. There is thus an urgent need to bring military preparations for coalition operations into line with the political weight placed on such arrangements.

This paper examines the role of coalitions in the defence strategies of the UK, France, Germany and the US; the performance of the Allies in multinational operations in the 1990s; and their planning for future coalitions. All of the major Allies recognise the importance of coalitions to their ability to use military power. However, political, budgetary and military constraints have meant that they have taken insufficient steps, both individually and through NATO, to ensure adequate preparation for multinational operations. The actual conduct of three of the major Western actions of the 1990s – in the Gulf, Bosnia-Herzegovina and Kosovo – has revealed specific disparities in the capabilities of the Allies, differences in doctrine and deficiencies in combined pre-crisis planning and coordination. In terms of future operations, three issues will be key: the impact of the broader transformation in warfare; the roles of NATO and the European Union (EU) in preparing forces for future operations, as well as non-institutional approaches; and the changing nature of coalitions themselves. Unless the Allies harmonise their approaches to these three critical issues, their ability to form effective coalitions will only decline.

Chapter 1

Coalitions and National Defence Strategies

National defence strategies and Allied force preparations in peacetime will determine how effective coalitions are in war. The core transatlantic Allies all acknowledge the strategic necessity of conducting military operations as part of multinational coalitions. However, each has found it difficult to make adequate preparations. The UK's standing military commitments and inadequate investment in personnel cast doubt on whether it can shoulder new coalition responsibilities. France's reluctance to engage in combined defence planning makes adequate preparation difficult. Germany, despite having Europe's largest armed forces, has been unable to make major military contributions to operations because of its political reluctance and lack of military readiness. Finally, the US has not sufficiently incorporated multinational contributions into its peacetime force preparations and operational planning, thereby necessitating an excessive reliance on *ad hoc* measures in a crisis.

The United Kingdom

The UK is the core Ally most inclined to operate as part of a coalition, and can almost seamlessly integrate with either US or other European forces. It has embraced coalition warfare as an organising principle for its defence, and has accepted a high degree of dependence on its Allies, especially the US. A central theme of the UK's Strategic Defence Review (SDR) of 1998 was the need to improve the British armed forces' capacity to intervene in distant contingencies in concert with international partners. The review noted that the 'need is increasingly to help prevent or shape crises further away and, if necessary, to deploy military forces rapidly before they get out of hand. Most force projection operations of this kind are likely to be multinational'.[1] Thus, under the SDR the UK plans to provide forces to meet two major, concurrent peace-support operations, or to fight a major regional conflict as part of a coalition, contributing forces roughly equal to those which it provided in the Gulf War of 1990–91: a reinforced heavy army division, a fighter wing and a naval carrier group.

London has assumed that its interests are most likely to be affected by events beyond Europe, for example in the Gulf or the Mediterranean region. As a Permanent Member of the UN Security Council, the UK also has a broader interest in maintaining international peace and security together with its closest strategic partners. These political considerations have translated into a defence posture that is optimised for expeditionary operations. The UK has therefore made projection capabilities – strategic transport aircraft and ships, aircraft carriers and lighter, more mobile forces – a priority.

The UK has implemented a number of reforms to strengthen its capacity for combined expeditionary operations. In 1999, it established the deployable Joint Rapid Reaction Forces (JRRF), modelled on the US joint-task-force concept which integrates ground, sea and air forces in peacetime for rapid deployment in a crisis. The JRRF should be fully operational in 2001. The British Army has been reorganised into two deployable divisions: the First Armoured Division composed of three armoured brigades, which will remain in Germany; and the Third Division, which will be based in the UK and will consist of an air-assault brigade and two mechanised brigades. The UK has also created a joint nuclear, biological and chemical (NBC) reconnaissance regiment to improve its forces' ability to conduct operations under NBC threat or attack. If they are fully implemented and funded, these organisational changes should provide the UK with ready forces to conduct two concurrent operations up to brigade level (approximately 4,600 troops each).

The UK is also improving its command-and-control capabilities, both to make operational planning easier during peacetime, and to deploy command elements rapidly in a crisis. Until the mid-

1990s, British expeditionary forces relied on *ad hoc*, single-service command arrangements. The UK could not undertake joint contingency planning, and had no pre-existing deployable joint-force headquarters, with its own communications and infrastructure. To remedy these deficiencies, a Permanent Joint Headquarters (PJHQ) was established in 1996, together with a new post of Chief of Joint Operations. The Chief of Joint Operations, who directs the PJHQ, is the main contingency planner in peacetime and operational commander of British forces in a crisis – comparable to a US regional commander-in-chief. The logistics components of the individual services have been brought together under a single, joint Chief of Defence Logistics.[2]

The SDR also launched a Joint Battle-space Digitisation Initiative, which will link together British land, sea and air forces.[3] The Royal Air Force (RAF) has adopted Mk 12 Identification Friend or Foe (IFF) transmitters and the *Have Quick* secure radio communications system – identical to the systems used by the US – in most of its combat aircraft.[4] The armed forces are also acquiring the Joint Tactical Information Distribution System (JTIDS)/Link 16 to ensure that data-links are interoperable with those of the US and other NATO Allies, and harmonising the UK's national Joint Operational Command System with the US Global Command and Control System.[5] Finally, the introduction of the advanced *Bowman* tactical digital radio system, one of the Army's priorities, will help British forces to operate with their 'digitised' US counterparts.[6]

In an attempt to meet the ambitious strategy outlined in the SDR, the UK increased defence spending in the 1998–99 fiscal year by £600 million, to £22 billion ($35bn). This rise followed a period of real decline in the budget between 1990 and 1997 of over 27%.[7] Compared with most of its NATO Allies, the UK's spending on equipment is relatively high, and that on personnel relatively low. In fact, the UK has maintained one of NATO's highest levels of procurement spending, averaging 25% of the defence budget between 1994 and 1998. Over the same period, military personnel costs averaged only 40% of the budget. Maintaining this ratio has, however, required politically difficult decisions, such as cutting the Territorial Army reserve force by 24% in 1998.[8] The emphasis on procurement has ensured that the UK remains in the first tier of nations in terms of military technology. However, it also casts doubt on whether the country's relatively small forces can meet an increasing number of overseas commitments.

Given the weight that the SDR placed on power projection, obtaining new transport ships and aircraft is a priority. While the UK has procured some of the transport and projection capabilities called for in the SDR, including two new landing platform docks (LPDs), a helicopter carrier and 25 C-130J theatre-transport aircraft, other key projection capabilities have not been acquired as planned.[9] The 1999 Defence White Paper concluded that the UK 'cannot at present deploy the JRRF quickly enough to meet the likely requirements of the new strategic environment'.[10] At the same time, long-standing but now less relevant programmes have continued. The UK has not modified its plans to acquire 232 *Eurofighters*, which are arguably much less central than strategic lift to the new British strategy.

Personnel shortages also cast doubt on whether British forces can meet the strategy set out in the SDR. In March 1999, then Defence Minister George Robertson stated that 35.6% of Army personnel were committed to operations abroad, and a further 20.4% were preparing for operational tours.[11] British Army and RAF personnel stationed overseas totalled 41,788 in 1999.[12] The UK also had 13,800 troops in Northern Ireland.[13] These prior commitments made it difficult for the UK to meet its original pledge to provide 12,000 personnel for the KFOR peacekeeping force in Kosovo, while also maintaining the regular rotation of its forces between deployments and home duty. Since the original build-up of 10,300 troops in June 1999, British forces in Kosovo had declined to around 4,000 by the end of the year. In December 1999, the Ministry of Defence announced that further reductions were planned.[14] By mid-2000, British forces in Bosnia will have been reduced by around 1,000, to 3,000 troops.[15] Forces have also been cut in other areas of the world, including the Gulf, where the British presence fell by 1,800 to less than 700 in 1999.[16] During the Kosovo conflict, the UK is reported to have offered 50,000 troops as part of a multinational force for a ground invasion, but it is doubtful whether it could have provided even half that number – or a force comparable to that which it provided for the Gulf War, and which the SDR called for as a requirement.[17] To muster 50,000 personnel, the UK would have needed to withdraw troops from garrisons and operations around the world, including Northern Ireland. The UK did not have the transport or logistical and medical support for a deployment of this size. Moreover, there were acute personnel shortages in speciality branches such as the Royal Signals, Royal Engineers and Army Medical Services.[18] According to a leaked British Army after-action report, shortages of equipment such as night-vision goggles, together with defective rifles and tactical radios, would have plagued the deployment.[19] These deficiencies indicate the difficulties that the UK might have confronted in the event of a ground war in Kosovo. More broadly, they also highlight the gap between current capabilities, and the SDR's requirements for power projection. The Chief of Joint Operations, Vice-Admiral Ian Garnett, has conceded that the British armed forces will not meet the SDR's requirements – designed specifically with Bosnia and Kosovo in mind – until they have recovered from their 'surge into the Balkans'.[20]

France

Although France mounted frequent small-scale interventions, mainly in Africa, it undertook no major expeditionary operations between the end of the Algerian war in 1962 and the 1991 conflict in the Gulf. The country's formal withdrawal from NATO's integrated military structure in 1966 meant that its armed forces did not have comprehensive experience of routine Alliance exercises, or of NATO doctrine and procedures governing the coordination and inter-operability of forces. Nevertheless, France did undertake some limited, *ad hoc* measures to increase interoperability with Allies in combined operations in Europe, such as developing Field Standing Operating Procedures agreed between the French II Corps and the US VII Corps.[21] In 1983, France established the Rapid Reaction Force (FAR), with sufficient strength for smaller-scale operations in sub-Saharan Africa, or to back up the French First Army with several divisions in the defence of West Germany. However, the FAR was under-funded and inadequate for large-scale outside interventions, while its reliance on conscripts and lack of strategic transport meant that it was incapable of truly rapid deployment.

The 1991 Gulf War revealed major deficiencies in French rapid-reaction forces and in the country's ability to operate effect-ively with its Allies, as well as exposing the more general inadequacy of French defence strategy. French forces were ill-suited for distant, high-intensity combat as part of a multinational force. Air force units found it difficult to make an effective contribution to the air campaign. Paris was reluctant to commit its most capable attack aircraft, the *Mirage* 2000, given its role in France's nuclear force.[22] Instead, it deployed *Mirage* F1s, which had significant operational drawbacks: they could not conduct night operations; they did not have anti-jam radios; and they risked being misidentified as Iraqi F-1s, which Baghdad had acquired before the war.[23] The *Daguet* light armoured division – totalling 12,000 men, cobbled together from disparate army units – was too light for close battle with front-line Iraqi forces. It also lacked sufficient interoperability with Allied forces to take part in the major thrust of the ground campaign, and so was assigned the task of defending the coalition's left flank when ground operations began in late February 1991. To compensate for its lack of organic fire support, an artillery brigade from the US 82nd Airborne Division was attached to the *Daguet* division. The navy, while playing an important part in enforcing the maritime embargo on Iraq, was essentially relegated to a logistical role, with the aircraft carrier *Clémenceau* shuttling helicopters and other cargo to the Gulf.

Following the Gulf War, France began a fundamental re-evaluation of its defence strategy. In a speech to the National Assembly in June 1991, then Minister of Defence Pierre Joxe outlined the main challenges the country faced:

> to improve the interoperability of our equipment with that of our principal allies, to act in Europe and outside Europe; to harden our power-projection forces and increase their reach and carrying capacity; to maintain the readiness and sufficiency of our stockpiles, notably for the most modern weapons; [and] to bring about a balance within our armed forces between conscription and professional soldiers, adapted to different types of operations.[24]

Joxe's defence manifesto provided the core themes of the 1994 Defence White Paper.[25] The White Paper noted that:

> After a period of expecting the major confrontation and preparing for it, the prevention and management of long crises of variable intensity is now our prevailing concern, requiring instruments that we do not always possess ...

> *Crises and operations more often than not take place at a significant distance from our national territory … Our facilities of prevention and action will be used, in a great majority of cases, in unison with our partners or allies, and in multinational groups.*[26]

This new defence strategy marked a dramatic departure from the last comprehensive review, the 1972 White Paper on National Defence. This had focused on protecting the territorial integrity of France and its approaches (West Germany and the Benelux countries), as well as its Overseas Departments and Territories, primarily by means of the French nuclear deterrent.[27] However, while the shift in French defence strategy towards regional conflicts and peace-support operations was a fundamental change, it did not imply the abandonment of the political principle underlying Gaullist strategy: achieving strategic independence and autonomy in security decision-making. The degree to which this principle can be reconciled with the realities of modern coalition operations abroad is a central tension in French security policy, and one which the 1994 White Paper did not resolve. Without greater peacetime coordination with its Allies, France risks becoming marginalised. However, coordination has a political cost: the potential subordination of French forces.

Throughout the 1990s, France tried to find its way between these two extremes. In 1996, it began structural reform – 'Model 2015' – to make its armed forces more effective in four main areas: deterrence, prevention, projection and protection. The importance accorded to projection capabilities and strategic intelligence has risen at the expense of the country's nuclear forces; as part of this reorientation, France has retired its land-based nuclear missiles. France's boldest reform came on 22 February 1996, when President Jacques Chirac announced the abolition of conscription. By 2003, when the transition to an all-regular military is scheduled to be complete, France plans to be able to deploy a force at least twice as large as the one that it sent to the Gulf: over 25,000 personnel for an engagement lasting 12–24 months, including plans for regular force rotations.[28] France has also made major changes to its military organisation, creating a Joint Forces Planning Staff (EMIA), an inter-service Directorate for Military Intelligence (DRM) and a deployable

Joint Theatre Command-and-Control Structure (PCIAT), comparable to similar structures in the US and Britain.[29]

As part of the 'Model 2015' structural reform, the navy will be reduced from 70,400 personnel to 56,500, and in a conflict will be able to deploy a naval air group. Air force personnel are to be cut from 94,000 to 70,000. The air force will be capable of deploying about 100 modern combat aircraft. The French army is undergoing the greatest changes of any of the services. The old structure, dividing forces between the FAR and the First Army, was replaced by the Land Action Force Command (CFAT) in 1998, which is charged with the operational planning for foreign deployments. By 2003, the army will have shrunk by around a third, from 270,000 personnel to 170,000, and will consist of 89 newly created regiments. These regiments will be grouped into 11 combat brigades: two armoured brigades, two mechanised brigades, two light armoured brigades, two infantry brigades, one airborne brigade, one reconnaissance brigade and France's contribution to the Franco-German Brigade.[30] According to Defence Minister Alain Richard, these changes aim to allow France 'to play an effective role in a coalition'.[31] The reorganisation has not, however, been without risk. Discussions of a possible ground invasion during the Kosovo conflict revealed the difficulties France faces in meeting its defence commitments until these changes are complete. According to the army, even by withdrawing its forces from Africa and the Overseas Departments and Territories, France could have supplied at most 10,000 troops for an invasion.[32] French commitments in Africa and in the Overseas Departments and Territories keep more than 15,000 personnel permanently mobilised, and even before the Kosovo war, 6,000 French troops were already in the Balkans.

In terms of capabilities, France places greatest emphasis on developing intelligence and data-processing systems. The *Helios* reconnaissance-satellite programme has continued, and *Horizon*, a helicopter-mounted wide-area ground-surveillance system utilising Moving Target Indicator (MTI) radar, has been introduced. France is developing new deployable command, control and communications systems to improve its ability to exchange information with coalition forces. It also plans to field new stand-off precision-guided munitions, and to acquire large transport aircraft.[33] In 1999, sea-trials began of the aircraft carrier *Charles de Gaulle*. The carrier will enter active service in 2001 to replace the *Foch*, which retires in 2000.

For France, finding the resources for its projection strategy will be difficult. Throughout the 1990s, tight budgetary constraints hampered attempts to restructure the military, and forced the cancellation of many prized, high-profile armaments programmes, such as the *Horus* synthetic aperture radar reconnaissance satellite, the *Zenon* signals-intelligence satellite and a replacement for the *Exocet* air-to-surface missile (ASM).[34] Reductions in French defence expenditure, while below the NATO average between 1994 and 1999, have nonetheless aggravated the problems inherent in achieving the interoperable, projection-oriented force described in the 1994 White Paper. Defence spending accounted for 3.3% of French gross domestic product (GDP) in 1994, declining to 2.15% by 1999. Procurement spending in particular has suffered to free up funds for the transition to all-regular personnel. The 1997–2002 Military Programme Law called for stabilising spending on equipment at FF85bn ($13bn) in constant 1998 francs. The government has, however, been unable to meet this target, and in 1999 reduced equipment spending by FF9.3bn ($1.45bn), or 10.8%.[35] Personnel costs rose from 51% of the budget in 1994 to 56% in 1998, while the proportion going on equipment and other expenditure fell from 49% to 44%.[36]

It is ultimately unclear whether France will be able to reconcile its guiding principles of strategic independence and autonomous decision-making with the greater peacetime coordination which is necessary if it is to become a major player in coalitions. Paris has traditionally eschewed standing commitments and peacetime integration to make its forces more readily available and to facilitate contingency planning for multinational operations. In the Gulf War, France did not commit its forces to offensive operations until the eve of the air campaign, which meant that its contribution was not included in earlier coalition planning. In preparing for the NATO-led Implementation Force (IFOR) deployment to Bosnia, there were difficulties in coordinating planning between France, which does not participate in the Alliance's integrated military structure, and the Supreme Headquarters Allied Powers in Europe (SHAPE). In Kosovo, the refusal of French air forces to execute certain missions

Table 1 Defence Expenditure by Country, 1993–2005

(1999 US$m)	1993	1994	1995	1996	1997	1998	1999	2000	2001	2002	2003	2004	2005
US	338,120	320,508	301,474	288,441	287,474	279,702	283,096	284,248	288,588	284,650	288,723	291,210	295,834
As % of GDP	4.5	4.1	3.8	3.5	3.3	3.1							
France	48,384	49,390	51,848	49,314	42,975	40,834	37,893	36,817	36,534	36,540	36,546	36,551	36,556
	3.4	3.3	3.5	3.3	3.0	2.8							
Germany	42,249	40,420	44,659	41,435	34,558	33,802	31,117	30,281	29,568	28,932	28,850	28,771	28,695
	1.9	1.8	2.0	1.8	1.6	1.5							
UK	39,831	38,705	36,722	37,079	36,799	38,093	35,940	36,092	35,605	35,525	35,281	35,192	35,106
	3.7	3.4	3.0	3.0	2.7	2.8							

Note Figures from 2001 are projected.
Source IISS Military Database

led to their temporary removal from the NATO air tasking order (ATO), which assigned strike missions to national forces. Retaining independent control over its national military forces has tended to increase French diplomatic leverage in the run-up to a conflict, but this has frequently come at the expense of influence over operational decisions. While in the past, France could reserve its decision about whether to participate in the defence of the West German frontier, adding its forces as a strategic reserve, modern operations demand a much greater level of integration, not only for effective action, but also to ensure that French influence is commensurate with its ambitions.

Germany

Germany is at once the core Ally most dependent on operating in coalitions, and the one most reluctant to take military action beyond its borders.[37] It is inconceivable that Germany would use force abroad unilaterally. The country has made progress in overcoming the burden of its history and its strong political reluctance to use force overseas in unison with its Allies. However, major constraints remain in terms of strategy, lack of political consensus and limited resources. Throughout the Cold War, Germany had no national military doctrine distinct from NATO's, nor did it possess a joint operational command structure for controlling its forces in non-NATO coalitions abroad. Even now the Cold War has ended, the country's military structure and ethos remain wedded to multi-national command, doctrine and organisation, and its approach to building a national military identity apart from NATO has been evolutionary, rather than revolutionary.

Germany maintains the 250,000-strong conscript-based Main Defence Forces (HVK) for territorial defence, while at the same time trying to build the smaller, largely professional Crisis Reaction Forces (KRK) for missions beyond its borders. The 1994 Defence White Paper explained that territorial defence would still take priority, but that Germany would also develop a modest capability for overseas missions:

> Germany's defence policy is based on a capability to conduct national defence, and to defend its allies as a form of extended national defence. It is supplemented by the ability to

> *participate in co-operative multinational conflict prevention and crisis management. German security policy is determined by the holistic combination of two basic functions: protection against risks and threats and the active shaping of stability and peace.*[38]

Since 1990, Germany has participated in 23 UN, Organisation for Security and Cooperation in Europe (OSCE) and NATO operations, including deployments to Turkey in 1991, Somalia in 1993, Bosnia from 1996 and Kosovo from 1999. In 1994, the Federal Constitutional Court affirmed that the country's Basic Law permitted the deployment of the *Bundeswehr* abroad, as long as parliamentary approval was given. The ruling removed doubts about whether overseas missions were compatible with Germany's Basic Law, and made the use of forces in armed missions overseas a purely political matter.

The KRK is central to efforts to enhance Germany's ability to participate effectively in coalition operations abroad. The force should number over 50,000 army and air force personnel by the end of 2000. The army element will consist of six fully equipped brigades (two armoured, one airborne, one light infantry, one air mechanised, and Germany's contribution to the Franco-German Brigade), each with three combat battalions.[39] The air force component will comprise 18 squadrons (two fighter squadrons, one suppression of enemy air defence (SEAD) squadron, one reconnaissance squadron, two air-defence squadrons and 12 ground-based air-defence squadrons composed of surface-to-air missile (SAM) units and radar systems), and three transport wings.[40] Approximately 40% of the German navy's ships participate in the KRK at any one time.[41]

Germany is also adapting its command structures and doctrine. It established a Joint Operational Command Centre (FüZBw) in 1995, comparable to the UK's PJHQ, to control its forces in combined operations. In 1999, the *Bundeswehr* released its first national Joint Operations Doctrine, supplementing NATO doctrine and focusing on the challenges of coalition operations abroad. To improve its ability to communicate with the US and other NATO Allies, Germany plans to acquire the Multifunctional Information Distribution System (MIDS).

However, Germany still lags behind the other core Allies. It faces the tightest fiscal and political constraints on preparing for overseas deployments, coordinating plans with its Allies and funding a deployable and sustainable force. Although legal doubts have been removed, the political consensus on dispatching forces abroad remains fragile. Germany is uncomfortable with the concept of 'projection', since this implies offensive operations, and is the most reluctant of the major Allies to earmark forces for out-of-area contingencies. Nevertheless, across the political spectrum there is growing acceptance of Germany's new role in regional security. A RAND study in 1995 found that an overwhelming majority of Germans supported involvement in multinational peacekeeping operations, although they remained opposed to using the *Bundeswehr* in combat missions.[42] A clear majority of Germans also oppose in principle deploying the *Bundeswehr* outside of NATO Europe.[43]

Germany also faces financial restrictions stemming from the costs associated with unification with the former East Germany and constraints imposed in order to meet the Maastricht Treaty criteria for fiscal deficits and government debt. Since 1990, the defence budget has been reduced by over 25% in real terms.[44] As a share of GDP, spending fell from around 3% in 1990 to 1.53% in 1998; of the NATO states, only Belgium, Canada, Luxembourg and Spain spend a smaller proportion of GDP on defence.[45] Even in the aftermath of the Kosovo war, when all quarters in Europe acknowledged the need to do more in defence, the *Bundeswehr* faced a new round of budget cuts as part of an overall austerity package. In June 1999, the government announced its intention to reduce the level of defence spending in the previous administration's mid-term financial plan for 2000–2005 by DM18.6bn ($10bn). In the 2000 budget alone, spending will be cut from DM48.3bn to DM45.3bn, a decrease of more than 6%. The defence budget will be further reduced to DM44.8bn in 2001, DM44.5bn in 2002 and DM43.7bn in 2003.[46] Between 1985 and 1998, the *Bundeswehr*'s share of the federal budget fell from 19% to 10.3%.[47]

With more than 60% of defence spending committed to more-or-less fixed personnel costs, the largest budget cuts have come in discretionary procurement accounts.[48] Between 1990 and 1997, the procurement budget fell from DM12bn ($7.05bn) to DM5.3bn. Over the same period, military expenditure for research and development declined from DM3.3bn to DM2.6bn.[49] This has meant that the

Bundeswehr has found it increasingly difficult to keep up with the modernisation programmes of Germany's core Allies. In 1996, a *Bundeswehr* study, *Employment of Armed Forces in 2020*, emphasised the importance of coalition operations and stressed the need to keep abreast of the technical and conceptual developments of the major Allies. The study placed particular emphasis on developing a 'system of systems', linking improved intelligence and surveillance capabilities with state-of-the-art information processing, communications and the means for precision strikes.[50] It is, however, unclear how influential this assessment has been within the Federal Ministry of Defence; under current plans, a decision on the radical modernisation suggested in the study will be postponed until at least 2010.[51]

While Germany is unlikely to adopt more advanced military systems, it continues to honour out-dated procurement decisions which, for political reasons, cannot easily be changed. Earlier commitments to procure the *Eurofighter*, *Leopard* 2 upgrades and Type 124 frigates – more relevant to border and coastal defence than to projecting power abroad – remain on track. Maintaining the procurement schedules for these programmes has come at the expense of other capabilities more urgently required for effective long-range operations. For example, although the 1994 White Paper called for four B-707 transports to be converted into refuelling aircraft – one of the air force's most serious deficiencies – Germany has acquired no tankers and remains dependent on its Allies. In the face of further budget cuts, Germany does not anticipate introducing a new fleet of strategic transport aircraft until 2010.[52]

Germany's experiences in Bosnia and Kosovo made clear the need to increase both the size and the capabilities of the KRK. There are severe shortages of communications specialists, logisticians and medical personnel. In an effort to alleviate these problems, Defence Minister Rudolf Scharping announced in July 1999 that 13,000 soldiers would be transferred from the HVK to the KRK, bringing its end-strength to 63,000.[53] However, Germany can neither fully resource an adequately large and well-equipped crisis-reaction force, nor avoid the 'hollowing' of its main defence force, which already suffers from substantial shortfalls in training, ammunition and spare parts for tanks and aircraft.[54] As analyst Franz-Josef Meiers has warned: 'In its present state – oversized and chronically underfinanced – the *Bundeswehr* will inevitably become a hollow force ill-suited for coping with wider security tasks and ill-prepared to preserve its interoperability with major NATO Allies'.[55]

These difficulties have driven Germany to re-evaluate the composition and structure of its forces. There is growing agreement between those who wish to reform the *Bundeswehr* so that it can act in coalition operations abroad, and those who seek greater savings in defence. Financial constraints have made military reform more pressing, and have forced the *Bundeswehr* to place greater emphasis on the KRK.[56] The real question, therefore, is how far Germany will go.

Considerable savings could be made by reducing the *Bundeswehr*'s manning levels. Dieter Lutz from the University of Hamburg argues that at least DM7bn a year could be saved, without loss of combat effectiveness, by reducing the size of the military to 200,000 professional soldiers, thereby moving away from a robust territorial defence.[57] This could be a more attractive proposition following NATO's enlargement in 1999 to include the Czech Republic, Poland and Hungary, which has given Germany the luxury of strategic depth for the first time in its modern history. In March 1999, Scharping observed that:

> *After NATO's enlargement our country is in a historically unprecedented good situation. We export security and stability. This, however, also makes our responsibility grow. Just think of the borders that our Alliance has, also with Iraq, Iran, or Syria. Common security and our contribution to this remain the central task; national defence seems to be less urgent nowadays.*[58]

Germany can now afford to transfer resources from the HVK to the KRK, thereby making it better able to meet threats to the security of NATO's new members, as well as crises further afield. According to General Peter Carstens, the chairman of the government's defence review, the Commission on the Future of the *Bundeswehr*, significant German participation in future coalitions will necessitate trebling the size of the KRK's army element to an end-strength of over 100,000.[59] Such an increase would probably entail large reductions in the HVK, if not its outright elimination, thereby undermining the central military rationale for conscription. Foregoing a large force structure for territorial defence would be controversial, both for political and for broader social reasons, and the government is unlikely to abolish conscription completely, although its precise terms are likely to change substantially. To a large extent, Germany's ability to participate more effectively in coalition operations will hinge on the outcome of this defence review and the orientation it adopts. If the government chooses to maintain conscription, and thus large forces, the challenge will be to make them relevant to the new missions that the *Bundeswehr* will be called upon to undertake – in other words, to turn its size to advantage. Whereas the UK and France will be better able rapidly to deploy combat forces in coalition operations, Germany's contributions may become the most sustainable, given its forces' larger rotational base. With plans for 200,000 professional soldiers available for out-of-area deployments, Germany could sustain up to a 40,000-strong force overseas, thereby allowing the country to assume much greater responsibilities in long-term peace-support operations.

The United States

The US finds it politically difficult to take unilateral military action. At the same time, coalitions are widely perceived by the country's military and the general public as restricting US freedom of action in conducting operations. This paradox helps to explain US defence planners' ambivalence as to how they view coalitions, and in how they prepare for them. The US Department of Defense's Quadrennial Defense Review (QDR) in 1997 underscored the importance of coalitions:

> While the United States will retain the capability to act unilaterally, a strategy that emphasizes coalition operations is essential to protecting and promoting our national interests ... Acting in coalition ... generally strengthens the political legitimacy of a course of action and brings additional resources to bear, ensuring that the United States need not shoulder the political, military, and financial burden alone.[60]

Although it made clear that the US would, if necessary, defend its vital interests unilaterally, the QDR also stressed that coalitions would be a likely precondition for military action in defence of lesser interests. It thus directed the US military to 'plan, train, and prepare to respond to the full spectrum of crises in coalition with the forces of other nations'.[61]

Several important steps have been taken to achieve this. In 1998, Secretary of Defense William Cohen proposed a Defence Capabilities Initiative (DCI) to improve the capacities of all NATO Allies in precision engagement, strategic mobility, logistics, force protection and communications, and to harmonise US and European operational styles. The Defense Department has redesigned a number of Advanced Concept Technology Demonstration (ACTD) programmes to encourage Allied participation in the development of advanced technologies.[62] It has also placed greater emphasis on interoperability in its acquisition process by requiring up-front assessments of the impact of new systems on the United States' ability to operate with its Allies.

These steps notwithstanding, the US military has generally not followed the QDR's guidelines in its preparations for coalition operations. According to a 1999 Defense Science Board study, the US has not paid enough attention to coalition issues in its planning, and has relied too much on 'ad hocery' in the formation, management and execution of multinational operations.[63] The study also noted that there is no comprehensive or systematic effort to integrate coalition considerations into US defence strategy.

Part of the problem lies with the strategy itself, which requires US forces to be able to fight and win, unilaterally if necessary, two nearly simultaneous major theatre wars. This has led the services to defend their current force structures and acquisition programmes as necessary if they are to prevail on their own, and discourages military planners from taking Allied contributions into account. Potential contributions are seen as additions to, rather than substitutes for, US forces and capabilities. But, as David Gompert and Richard Kugler have observed, 'As long as we choose not to depend on Allies, we will fail to make the joint preparations needed to ensure effective coalition operations'.[64]

Doubts about the reliability of its Allies, both in terms of their political willingness to participate and their military capabilities, are another reason why the US has not made long-term preparations for coalition operations. Whereas during the Cold War, the contributions of the European NATO Allies could be safely relied upon in planning for a conflict that would probably be fought on their own territory, this discipline has now gone, and their participation in a coalition with the US beyond Europe is open to question. While European countries have their own doubts about the reliability of the US as a coalition partner, in the absence of an autonomous defence capability they have resigned themselves to accepting the risks. In contrast, US concerns about the unreliability of others tend to reinforce its efforts to maintain a capacity for unilateral action.

With the exception of war plans related to the defence of Europe, European Allies see little of US operational planning, or of its joint exercise programme outside of Europe. They are generally not included in US planning until they have committed to participate in an operation, but by then it may be too late for them to influence it. The more the US plans for unilateral operations, the more marginal its Allies will become, thereby strengthening arguments against acting in concert with the US. The reverse may, however, also be true. If the US took greater account of coalition contributions in its defence strategy and planning, and even accepted a real dependence on its Allies for accomplishing some missions, Allied participation may become more reliable, and coalitions more cohesive.

The perceived tension between acting in a coalition and maintaining America's global military superiority is a final inhibition on US preparations. US academics, policy-makers and industry leaders appear to place equal value on these two foreign-policy goals: in a poll by the Chicago Council on Foreign Relations in 1999, 58% of respondents saw each as 'very important'.[65] However, US defence strategy has given priority to maintaining military dominance. To do so at a time when threats, technologies and styles of war are changing demands the rapid introduction of new military technologies, the development of innovative operational concepts and the reconfiguration of military organisations. There is broad consensus in the US, represented in the conclusions of the independent National Defense Panel of 1997, as well as in the QDR, that change is necessary if the country is to meet potential long-term threats, such as conflict with China, or with a coalition of hostile regional powers.[66] While this goal takes precedence, there is also a growing acknowledgement that it may make it harder for the US to operate in coalitions.

This perceived tension is not, however, a simple choice between either accelerating military reforms or slowing them down to allow more cash-strapped Allies to catch up. Greater reliance on coalitions may in fact make military reform easier. The United States' ability to transform its military is hampered by the costs of current operations and of maintaining its large force structure, as well as the costs of replacing rapidly ageing equipment. A report in 1999 by the Center for Strategic and International Studies concluded that, between fiscal years 1997 and 2015, the Department of Defense may face an annual spending shortfall of $100bn just to maintain the force structure outlined in the QDR.[67] Although this figure has been widely challenged, there is a growing consensus in Washington that the Department of Defense is underspending by at least $25bn.[68] Wider pressures on the federal budget, such as the need for increased expenditure on the elderly and on education, as well as calls for lower taxes, suggest that any increase in investment is more likely to come from cuts in forces and in current operations, than from significantly higher overall funding for the Department of Defense.

If the US does move to a smaller force structure, reduce its operational costs and allocate greater resources to redesigning its forces, it will have to rely more on coalitions. A smaller military, Eliot Cohen has suggested, 'will have to concede that some missions are simply too big for it to handle alone. Indeed, one of the chief strategic choices that the United States faces is that between unilateral and multilateral capabilities'.[69] This would require the much greater integration of potential coalition contributions and requirements into US force planning, as well as allowing the Allies a role akin to South Korea's in peacetime operational planning. Planning for crisis-response operations is more complex and involves greater uncertainty than it does for collective defence. Realising the potential savings from multinational planning will entail substantial risks for the US, complicate its war preparations and make command in a crisis more cumbersome. Nevertheless, overcoming these obstacles and truly integrating coalition considerations into US defence planning could play a key role in enabling the US military to meet future threats. It would also improve the overall health of the transatlantic relationship. The challenge will be identifying what the US is prepared to give up, and how far it is willing to rely on its Allies.

America's vital strategic interests, especially the defence of its homeland, will continue to demand a unilateral capability. The level of preparation for contingencies in which US vital interests are not at stake is variable, and more discretionary. In cases such as these, or where its interest is arguably less than that of its Allies, the US could be more inclined to operate in a coalition, and indeed to depend on multinational approaches. The US could follow the lead of its major European Allies and take account of their resources in determining its own national contributions, especially for smaller-scale operations. Thus, coalitions would become a military, as well as a political, precondition for US involvement in crises that do not affect vital strategic interests, while freeing up resources that the country needs to meet longer-term threats beyond Europe.

All of the core transatlantic Allies understand that efforts must be made to improve their performance in combined operations. However, each faces substantial political, budgetary, institutional and structural obstacles. These constraints are unlikely to be overcome quickly. If the Allies are to improve their preparations for coalitions, the impetus is likely to come, not from national defence strategies themselves, but from the lessons learnt from the coalition operations of the 1990s.

Chapter 2

Transatlantic Coalitions in the 1990s

The Gulf War and operations in Bosnia and Kosovo have demonstrated both the types of challenges faced by modern coalitions, and how the Western style of war is changing the way in which the effectiveness of coalitions is measured. These three cases also highlight the disparities in the capabilities of the coalition partners, the uneven levels of prior coordination and the inevitable political and military frustrations that multinational operations involve. Above all, they show that the greatest strategic threat for Western coalitions is not their defeat in battle, but the gradual erosion of their cohesion. Successful operations require more than unity of purpose at the outset; they also necessitate greater pre-crisis preparation and more complementary contributions from all members. While the coalitions in the Gulf, Bosnia and Kosovo succeeded despite *ad hoc*, 'come as you are' approaches, these may prove insufficient to meet the political and military demands of future conflicts.

The Gulf War and the Challenges of Force Projection

The multinational coalition that formed to reverse Iraq's invasion of Kuwait in August 1990 was one of the most successful in recent history. It coalesced around the US, which provided more than two-thirds of the coalition's ground, air and naval forces. The dominant US role in forming the coalition and in planning and commanding it was vital to ensuring that the mission succeeded, but also created friction that could have undermined political cohesion had Iraq offered greater resistance.

Combined Planning and Command

The Gulf War followed a long tradition in coalition operations whereby the leader calls the tune: while the US consulted closely with its core Allies throughout the crisis, it retained the prerogatives of command and controlled the planning process. There was no question that ultimate authority rested with the US president. The US conducted extensive, unilateral contingency planning before Iraq's invasion of Kuwait, and in the build-up to the counter-offensive, with little or no Allied military involvement until the last stages of preparation.[1] Even key Allied heads of state had little access to detailed planning and were only notified of the United States' decision to begin the offensive immediately prior to the start of the air campaign in January 1991 (British Prime Minister John Major received 12 hours' notice, French President François Mitterrand less than one).[2]

In contrast with the level of US pre-planning for a war with Iraq, none of the core European Allies had national contingency plans for conflicts in the Persian Gulf. France, the UK and Germany all lacked the pre-existing command structures and staff to create such plans, or to form the nucleus of any national contribution to a multinational expeditionary force. In practice, this meant that their expeditionary forces were formed piecemeal, under national commanders who were only chosen, and who only began planning, after the crisis erupted. This lack of specific pre-planning was only partially mitigated after the crisis began. In late 1990, multinational forces joined the Coalition Coordination, Communication and Integration Centre and, by the end of the year, British RAF officers had joined the secretive 'Black Hole' staff cell responsible for targeting and mission planning for the air campaign.[3] France played no role in the planning process, largely as a result of political decisions taken before the conflict. Paris originally insisted that its aircraft would only be used in support of French ground forces, and agreed only to attack targets in Kuwait, not in Iraq. These positions were swiftly modified after the resignation of Defence Minister Jean-Pierre Chevènement on 29 January 1991.[4]

The fact that planning remained largely unilateral ensured a plan that was strategically coherent and militarily effective. But it was also politically unsatisfactory to major Allies such as France, which was frustrated by its lack of influence and by its dependence on US strategic intelligence and command structures. There was a clear correlation between military capability and political clout. The UK, which contributed over 35,000 personnel, had much greater influence over the course of the operation than either France, which contributed less than half as many troops, or Germany, which did not participate militarily but made a substantial financial contribution to the war effort.[5]

Multinational Doctrine

The Gulf War coalition benefited from NATO's war-fighting doctrine, and the doctrinal cohesion of Alliance members – with the notable exception of France – was high.[6] Through NATO, the Allies had gained confidence and mutual trust. Allied military commanders had held positions in NATO's military command, and had forged personal relationships with their counterparts from other countries. They had become familiar with national idiosyncrasies and operational styles. All of these experiences served them well in the Gulf.

By 1991, NATO's operational concept Follow-On Forces Attack (FOFA) had lost its relevance in terms of a conflict with the Warsaw Pact. It was, nevertheless, ideal as a common frame of reference for the Gulf War campaign, with its emphasis on coordinated air and ground attacks in depth against an extended adversary's armoured forces. The concept also exploited the coalition's comparative advantage of manoeuvre and coordination between services. While FOFA was criticised in the 1980s for its dependence on unproven technologies, such as Joint Surveillance Target Attack Radar System (JSTARS) ground-surveillance aircraft, it came of age with the Gulf War, in which many of these technologies reached operational fruition.[7] The Gulf conflict would, however, be both the first and last in which FOFA could be applied with any relevance. Beyond the increasingly distant possibility of a sequel, the age of force-on-force tank battles ended with the coalition's overwhelming victory.

Beyond common doctrine, NATO's combat and logistics exercises were ideal preparation for the large-scale deployment of forces to the Gulf.[8] Annual NATO exercises such as *Reforger* involved over 80,000 Allied troops and the simulated and actual movement of massive forces from the US to Europe, coupled with realistic, large-scale field exercises. In addition, a number of Allied air forces participated in the US *Red Flag* combat exercises at Nellis Air Force Base, Nevada, prior to the Gulf War. One British veteran of the Gulf conflict complimented the exercises on their rigour and realism, half-jokingly claiming that the Gulf War 'was the best practise for *Red Flag*' that his squadron had ever had.[9]

Key Capabilities

In contrast with the relevance of NATO's doctrine, exercises and other preparations, the Gulf conflict revealed major deficiencies in coalition capabilities, particularly those related to long-range force projection. Whereas the Cold War obliged the US to develop these capabilities, it compelled European forces to plan for the territorial defence of Western Europe. The Gulf War revealed particularly significant gaps between US and European capabilities in four areas: intelligence, surveillance and reconnaissance; precision attack; transport; and force protection.

Intelligence, Surveillance and Reconnaissance

The Gulf War highlighted the discrepancy between the theatre and, especially, strategic intelligence capabilities of the US, and those of the major European Allies. During the war, French leaders claimed that they were almost completely dependent on the US, undermining one of the central tenets of Gaullist security policy – strategic autonomy. Defence Minister Joxe conceded that: 'It was the United States that furnished us, when and as they chose to do so, with the essential information necessary for the conduct of the conflict'.[10] The Gulf War revealed the full breadth of US capabilities: the role its satellites played in surveillance as well as early-warning of ballistic-missile launches; and the flexibility and variety of its reconnaissance aircraft and drones, and other means of collecting militarily relevant information.

Precision Attack

Concerns about collateral damage and the risk to aircrews prompted a much greater reliance than hitherto on 'smart' weapons. While precision-guided munitions were used in the final days of the Vietnam War, the Gulf conflict demonstrated their new pre-dominance in the way that the West uses force. In addition to the US, both France and the UK had some precision-guided munitions, such as the AS-30 and *Martel*.[11] However, the stocks of all the major Allies were insufficient.

Transport

The conflict also demonstrated the need for long-range transport, and the disparity in US and European capabilities in this area. Only the US had enough aircraft and ships to move multiple divisions to the Gulf quickly. Its major European partners, by contrast, were largely dependent on commercial shipping and aviation. They also had only limited numbers of theatre-transport aircraft. At the time of the war, the UK had three *Tristar* C-2s, 13 VC-10 C-1s and 60 C-130s; France 70 C-160 Transalls, ten C-130s and six DC-8s; and Germany 84 C-160s and four Boeing 707s. In contrast, the US had 110 C-5 and 250 C-141 strategic-transport aircraft, as well as three times as many theatre-transport aircraft (520 C-130s and 12 C-135s). It had many more aerial-refuelling aircraft than its European Allies (591 KC-135s and 57 KC-10s, compared with the UK's 12 *Victors*, four *Tristar* K-1s, two Tristar KC-1s, five VC-10 K-2s and four K-3s, and France's 11 C-135F/FRs). Germany had (and still has) no aerial-refuelling aircraft at all.[12] In addition, the European Allies lacked sufficient roll-on, roll-off transport ships to move heavy forces quickly to the Gulf. The benefits of having all-regular personnel were also clear: the UK deployed its 35,000-strong contingent faster and more easily than France did its 13,500 troops. Although the French forces deployed to the Gulf were largely professional, it was difficult to pull them out of units which comprised both professionals and conscripts, who cannot under French law be sent on overseas missions. This lesson was key to France's 1996 decision to abolish conscription, and became a central argument in the debate on conscription in Germany.

Force Protection

The rear-area and friendly-fire casualties suffered by the coalition in the Gulf War underscored the need to improve force protection and combat identification. Iraq's ballistic missiles, coupled with its arsenal of chemical and biological weapons (although never used against coalition forces), drew attention to how deficient the coalition was in protective measures. None of the Allies had sufficient stocks of lightweight protective suits, adequate vaccines and other medical countermeasures, deployable collective protection, non-aqueous decontamination systems suitable for desert conditions, or reliable detection systems. The coalition's reliance on local civilians to unload cargo at ports and airfields, as well as to transport supplies to forward operating bases overland, meant that the threat of a chemical or biological attack could have significantly disrupted the build-up to the offensive. Coupled with the faster, non-linear style of the campaign, the presence of coalition forces with different types of equipment and the possibility of misidentification led to a number of friendly-fire incidents.[13] On 26 February 1991, for example, a US aircraft mistakenly attacked a British armoured personnel carrier, killing nine soldiers.[14]

Perhaps the most important lesson regarding force protection is that the Gulf War is likely to prove an anomaly. Coalitions cannot assume that they will be given, as they were in the Gulf, unimpeded access to a theatre and a long period of time to acclimatise their forces before their integration into a coalition for combat. Thus, national forces must be able to protect themselves, integrate into a coalition prior to deployment and fight their way into a theatre. If their national forces cannot adequately defend themselves while entering a theatre, political leaders may be less willing to commit them to a coalition operation. Unprotected forces sent on expeditionary operations could complicate campaign planning. Other Allies could be required to reallocate resources for their protection, and to accept a disproportionate share of missions and tasks. At worst, the political benefits of a country joining a coalition may be outweighed by the military liabilities of operating with forces that cannot adequately protect themselves. As a result, throughout the 1990s the core transatlantic Allies, especially the US and the UK, placed more emphasis on ensuring the survivability of their forces and their capacity to sustain operations under chemical or biological attack.

Bosnia and the Challenges of Peace Support

US and European experiences in Bosnia reinforced many lessons of the Gulf War, but also broadened the list to reflect the challenges of long-term peacekeeping operations. Many of the operational decisions NATO made regarding IFOR were coloured by the experience of the earlier UN Protection Force (UNPROFOR). UNPROFOR's muddled and complex 'dual-key' command arrangements demonstrated the political and military difficulties inherent in bifurcated commands, while restrictive rules of engagement further limited its freedom of action. UNPROFOR's problems also underscored the importance of dispatching capable combat forces, even for peacekeeping operations. As then British Defence Minister Robertson put it in March 1999: 'to be the best at peacekeeping, you need first to be the best at war-fighting. It is no coincidence that when NATO deployed tanks, armoured vehicles and artillery pieces to Bosnia, the parties took note of our determination and opted for peaceful co-existence'.[15]

Unlike in the Gulf, during the run-up to NATO's intervention in Bosnia in December 1995 there were fundamental political disagreements between the US and its European Allies over the origins of the conflict, the degree of security interests affected and the proper role of military force to end the fighting. Five months before IFOR's deployment in December 1995, as UNPROFOR began to wind down, the emerging US–European coalition seemed to be unravelling even before it had begun. There was a fundamental difference of view between the US, which had no forces on the ground in Bosnia, and its closest European Allies, which had made the largest contributions to UNPROFOR and were therefore most vulnerable to renewed violence. The US Senate's vote in July 1995 to lift the arms embargo against the Bosnian Muslims met with consternation in Europe. European nations opposed lifting the embargo on the grounds that doing so would destroy UNPROFOR's posture of impartiality and lead to Serb reprisals. According to the prevalent European view, 'Without the risks being shared on the ground, the efforts of the Europeans would always be at the mercy of a change in US policy'.[16] Subsequently, therefore, US forces were deployed in the Balkans as much for political as for military reasons.

Combined Planning and Command

Contingency planning for a NATO intervention began in mid-1994. Early preparations focused on devising a plan to deploy a large NATO force to assist, if necessary, in UNPROFOR's evacuation from Bosnia. This served as the basis for NATO's ultimate deployment of forces. Despite disagreements at the political level, these preparations were marked by a high degree of multinational participation and coordination. The NATO-led coalition benefited both from the identification of the US as the lead nation in IFOR (it contributed about half of the coalition's total strength of approximately 50,000 troops), and from the prior presence in Bosnia of British, French and other European personnel. Through their UNPROFOR experience, these troops were already familiar with local conditions, and could be quickly inserted into the new NATO command structure. The high degree of European participation in the planning for Bosnia fostered greater cohesion than was the case in the Gulf, or would be in Kosovo, and contributed to the reconciliation of US and European political positions.

Multinational Doctrine

In contrast with the relatively smooth planning process, IFOR suffered from the absence of an agreed multinational doctrine for peace-support operations. Instead, participating countries turned to their national doctrines. US, British, German and NATO doctrinal principles are almost identical, and those of France, while more distinct, are nonetheless compatible. However, there are key differences in how these principles have been applied.[17] The US, unlike France or the UK, has no distinct joint doctrine for peace-support operations. Instead, peacekeeping is addressed in the 1995 Joint Doctrine for Military Operations Other Than War, which also includes other disparate missions, such as arms control and combating terrorism.[18] The US puts relatively greater emphasis on protecting its forces, especially in conflicts where its vital strategic interests are not at stake. As Peter Feaver and Christopher Gelpi have observed:

> *In the Bosnian peacekeeping operation, casualty aversion reached an unprecedented level. 'Force Protection', meaning the prevention of US casualties, became an explicit mission goal, on par with, if not superseding, the primary mission of restoring peace to Bosnia. As a result, war criminals were not aggressively pursued and arrested, community-building activities were curtailed, and every stray movement of a US peacekeeper was a mission-threatening event.[19]*

The US seeks to minimise its 'footprint' within a theatre – its visible presence and the exposure of its forces – by isolating its forces in secure camps, refraining from interacting with locals and patrolling in a visibly self-protective manner. Some French analysts have cited US intolerance of casualties as evidence of its unreliability in peace-support operations.[20] The UK's Peace Support Operations Doctrine states that:

> *In general terms, resources dedicated to defensive purposes might be more usefully applied to developing the mission towards its end-state. The adoption of an overt defensive posture can have a negative effect upon the credibility of the force and any civil affairs programme. A fine line has to be drawn between effective defence and what might be perceived as an unnecessary 'bunker mentality'.*[21]

In conducting peace-support operations, all the transatlantic Allies aim to deter war and promote peace. The US, however, tends to place greater emphasis on preventing a conflict from re-igniting, first and foremost by remaining in a strong war-fighting posture. European countries, on the other hand, see the need to deter conflict, but have also been more willing to promote wider mission objectives, including by supporting other, non-military mission components, such as specialised UN agencies and non-governmental organisations. In Bosnia, British and French forces have been much more inclined to interact with local people and to conduct patrols with a much lower protective posture. Colonial experiences and the use of national militaries in constabulary-like missions – the British Army in Northern Ireland or French troops in North Africa, for example – have created a more flexible approach to peacekeeping.[22] The US lacks this kind of experience, and is unlikely ever to embrace peacekeeping to the same extent as its European Allies. Nonetheless, the shared lessons of the Balkan deployments are being learned. Since 1995, the peace-support doctrines of the major Allies have come closer together. In 1997, NATO updated its peace-support doctrine (MC 327/1) based on the lessons of IFOR.[23] There is a growing recognition in Washington that US military participation in multinational peacekeeping missions will remain necessary in the future. As US experience of this type of operation grows, its approach is likely to change, allowing a better balance to be struck between ensuring the security of its forces, and promoting core mission objectives.

Key Capabilities

The IFOR deployment, NATO's first-ever out-of-area operation, presented the Alliance with three major challenges, each of which demanded different types of capabilities. The first challenge was logistical. Despite Bosnia's relative proximity to NATO bases in Western Europe and to military facilities in Hungary, as well as the absence of high-intensity combat, deploying and staging forces there was extremely difficult. In addition, the local infrastructure – roads, the electricity grid, communications networks, water supplies and sewage treatment – had been almost completely destroyed. Lastly, no one knew how long NATO forces would remain in Bosnia. The second challenge facing the Alliance concerned communications, command and control, which was complicated by the involvement of a large number of non-NATO countries, including Russia and other former Warsaw Pact states, and by deficiencies in interoperable systems. Third, IFOR's mission to enforce the Dayton Peace Agreement required extremely good intelligence to monitor the movement and disarmament of the warring factions, track alleged war criminals and guard against terrorist attacks.

Logistics

The Bosnian operations demonstrated the need to improve NATO's logistics doctrine and capabilities. Alliance doctrine stipulates that deployment is a national responsibility; authority is not transferred to the local Alliance commander until after forces have arrived in the theatre. As Roger Palin has observed, 'The commander thus assumes command of his force in the early, potentially crucial, stages in piecemeal fashion'.[24] Treating deployment and logistics as national responsibilities was extremely inefficient in Bosnia, given the small size of many countries' force contributions and the failure to integrate forces into the coalition before they reached the theatre.[25] In future operations, US–European forces will be most vulnerable as they enter the theatre. The inadequacy of multinational deployment and command arrangements in the early phases of a conflict may therefore put an operation at risk. Its IFOR experience has prompted NATO to place greater emphasis on multinational logistics, establishing Multinational Joint Logistics Centres that could support either NATO or non-NATO combined joint task force operations.

IFOR also highlighted the difficulties that all the major Allies faced in sustaining a sizeable out-of-area operation over several years. The deployment was much smaller than the Western build-up in the Arabian desert in 1990 (roughly 50,000 troops in Bosnia, against 600,000 in the Gulf); it was the long-term commitment that posed the greatest challenge. After the initial deployment, force rotations every three to six months became necessary. The cycle of training for the mission, conducting it and recovering from it required three to five times the actual number of forces in theatre. Personnel shortages were especially acute among specialists such as signallers, combat engineers, linguists, civil-affairs officers and medical personnel, as well as logisticians.[26] Noting the difficulties NATO experienced, General Klaus Naumann, the former chairman of the NATO Military Committee, has warned that 'Sustainability is the Achilles' heel of the Alliance'.[27]

Communications, Command and Control

IFOR's communications, command and control benefited from preparations made before the force was deployed. In April 1995, NATO conducted a major interoperability trial, *Interop 95*, which revealed technical problems that could be fixed before the deployment. In addition, the absence of large-scale violence during the deployment and build-up of forces gave the Allies time to develop *ad hoc* solutions. This may not, however, be the case in future operations, thus making pre-planning and interoperability trials all the more important.

Despite the preparations made before deployment, IFOR still encountered significant communications, command and control problems. These do not suggest a major technological gap between US and European forces, but rather highlight the difficulties caused by inadequate prior agreement on common systems, interfaces and procedures. Since Bosnia had no working telephone system, the coalition was almost completely dependent on its own communications networks. Each of the major Allies had its own national theatre-communications systems. The US Tri-Service Tactical Mobile

Subscriber Equipment (TRI-TAC MSE) and the UK's *Ptarmigan* were fully interoperable via a digital interface. However, the US system was only interoperable with the French RITA and German *Autoko* systems through an older and less effective analogue interface, which slowed data transmission.[28] While STU-IIB secure telephones were approved for NATO and used by European forces, US troops had STU-III systems that were not easily interoperable.

Bosnia was also NATO's first operation in the information age, and forces faced the same types of problems as those which plague information systems in the commercial sector. Systems were vulnerable to computer viruses, and personnel often passed infected disks between unclassified and classified systems. According to one after-action study, in IFOR's first 60 days nearly every US Army computer brought into the theatre was infected with a virus. The classified Crisis Response Operations NATO Operating System (CRONOS) and other national systems were also infected.[29] Bosnia made clear that Western coalitions are particularly vulnerable to 'cyber attacks'; to prevent them, coalition forces will need to develop strict procedures to safeguard information systems, including enforcement mechanisms to ensure compliance.

Finally, information networks were unable to reach lower-echelon units. Systems such as the Linked Operations/Intelligence Centres Europe (LOCE) provided a common link between the major Allies for exchanging secret operational and intelligence information, but the network did not extend below the division level because lower-level units could not meet its technical requirements.[30] In addition, for some coalition states, controlling national forces required national control over the flow of information to tactical forces. In their view, it would be undesirable to extend strategic-level command and information, which could come from another country, down to the tactical level. Such national information channels could, however, make it difficult to achieve better performance in future coalitions.

Intelligence, Surveillance and Reconnaissance

When NATO deployed to Bosnia, it brought with it advanced intelligence, surveillance and reconnaissance capabilities. These played two major roles: they verified the relocation and disarmament of the warring factions; and they were crucial to detecting indications of renewed civil disorder or terrorist activity.[31] Airborne surveillance systems, which were originally developed with a major war in Europe in mind, were quickly adapted to meet these demands. JSTARS and unmanned aerial vehicles (UAVs) helped to verify troop withdrawals into the zones of separation in accordance with the Dayton agreement. Signals-intelligence and reconnaissance systems (including aircraft such as the US RC-135 *Rivet Joint*, France's C-160G *Gabriel*, French, Italian and German *Atlantiques* and British *Nimrods*) were indispensable in locating forces, tracking alleged war criminals and foiling terrorist attacks. In contrast with the Gulf War, in Bosnia JSTARS, UAVs and manned reconnaissance aircraft played a greater role than strategic assets such as satellites in informing political and operational decisions.

NATO was, however, short of trained intelligence analysts and linguists familiar with the Balkans. Sharing intelligence also posed a problem: it was difficult to establish a two-tier arrangement, whereby all participating nations (including Russia and other non-NATO states) could share one level of information, while NATO states would share another. Data carried by national intelligence-information systems could not easily be transferred between different systems; in many cases, this had to be done by hand. Above all, the timely sharing of information was stymied by out-dated release procedures. For all these reasons, NATO recognised the need to improve its intelligence capabilities and the procedures for sharing information.

Kosovo and the Challenges of Coercive Operations

On one level, the Kosovo conflict can only be viewed as a remarkable success: Belgrade capitulated, the Western coalition held together and there were no Allied combat casualties. The defensive North Atlantic Alliance accomplished an offensive mission – its first major, sustained combat operation. The accuracy of the weapons and the minimal collateral damage set new, albeit probably unrepeatable, standards for future combined operations.

Yet for many participants and observers, the campaign raised deeper concerns. To all intents and purposes, the US conducted the war on behalf of its European Allies, dominating both the operation's planning, and its execution. Throughout the conflict, there were doubts about whether the Yugoslav regime would ultimately comply with NATO's demands to withdraw from Kosovo. The Allies were in danger of losing cohesion had the conflict dragged on much longer than it did, since this would have forced a decision on a ground invasion. Several Allies, including Germany, Greece and Italy, opposed a ground intervention, and there was little enthusiasm for it in the US.[32] The lack of coordination between the major Allies on targeting before the air campaign began made decisions taken in the heat of battle more contentious. Parallel US and NATO command-and-control structures complicated the operation's planning and execution, while the absence of Allied casualties only reinforced the misguided belief in the West that war is becoming free of risk.

Kosovo revealed both the quantitative and qualitative disparities between the capabilities of the US, and those of Europe. The US accounted for approximately 60% of the 38,000 sorties flown during the conflict, and provided about two-thirds of the 900 aircraft involved.[33] Qualitatively, the gap was even wider. Only the US had stealth aircraft and all-weather, air-launched precision munitions. It also conducted the vast majority of the Alliance's strike-support sorties, such as command-and-control, surveillance, aerial refuelling and electronic warfare. The dominance of the US was resented in Europe, and gave rise to a desire in many capitals for greater strategic independence from Washington. This feeling was strongest in Paris. According to the after-action report of the French Ministry of Defence, 'the Kosovo crisis has increased our determination to grant the European Union the ability to decide, devise and carry out large-scale military operations'.[34] From the US side, as Deputy Secretary of State Strobe Talbott has warned:

> *Many Americans are saying: never again should the United States have to fly the lion's share of the risky missions in a NATO operation and foot by far the biggest bill. Many in my country – notably members of Congress – are concerned that, in some future European crisis, a similar predominance of American manpower, firepower, equipment and resources will be neither politically nor militarily sustainable, given the competing commitments our nation has in the Gulf, on the Korean Peninsula, and elsewhere around the world.*[35]

To restore the transatlantic partnership to health, these centrifugal political sentiments will need to be overcome. This will mean addressing comprehensively the challenges and problems revealed by Kosovo.

Combined Planning and Command

Planning and command in Kosovo were more complex and more cumbersome than in either the Gulf War or in Bosnia. The problems stemmed from NATO's miscalculation that a limited air campaign of two or three days would force the Yugoslav regime to capitulate. Thus, as the talks in Rambouillet broke down in March 1999, the Supreme Allied Commander Europe (SACEUR), General Wesley Clark, developed a two-day air-strike plan.[36] To meet this limited requirement, NATO had fewer than 220 targets, nearly half of which were exhausted in the first three days of the conflict.[37] Within the first week of bombing, it became clear that the campaign would be prolonged, and that NATO would need additional targets. But the Alliance did not have a broader set of targets for a protracted series of strike missions.

NATO's limited preparations were quickly overtaken by *ad hoc* measures. As the campaign went on, the responsibility for target selection and mission planning steadily shifted from NATO to the US joint task force *Noble Anvil*, which managed the US contribution to the campaign and controlled sensitive US assets, such as the B-2 and F-117 stealth aircraft, outside of NATO channels.[38] This essentially created two competing command structures, which occasionally worked at cross-purposes. While the target-approval process was multilateral, target selection remained almost entirely in US hands. As one senior NATO commander put it in July 1999: 'One should always train the way one plans to fight. In this case, however, NATO did not fight the way it trained. The [US joint task force] took over everything and left other nations watching from the sidelines'.[39] This was a major source of friction throughout the campaign.[40]

Target selection and approval was slow, opaque and fraught with political risks. Although Clark was ultimately given the authority to sanction most targets, those in politically sensitive Belgrade and Montenegro, or where high collateral damage was possible, required approval by Allied political leaders. European countries found it difficult to approve quickly targets which they had no hand in selecting, and where they had to rely on US estimates of collateral damage. These delays made it difficult for NATO to take the initiative. Often, targets were assigned to aircrews on the same day that they were to be attacked.[41] Ironically, this meant that some of the most politically sensitive targets received the least amount of mission planning.

Allied consultations during the conflict produced numerous disagreements.[42] The fundamental point of difference was between the US, which wanted to escalate the war by increasing the original target set some ten-fold, and the continental European states, which sought to avoid escalation – both in terms of the level of force and through widening the conflict to include neighbouring areas such as Montenegro – by ensuring that NATO's highest political body, the North Atlantic Council, retained direct control over the use of force.[43] After the war, French President Chirac portrayed his country's role in vetoing targets such as Belgrade bridges and sites in Montenegro not only as attempts to control the escalation of violence, but also as a demonstration of his country's 'capacity for independence'.[44] The UK and Germany also disagreed with the US over targeting. The UK allowed US B-52 bombers based at Fairford in England to be used only against airfields and other isolated military targets, so as to avoid collateral damage.[45] For the same reasons, Germany had reservations about targets proposed by the US in Belgrade and Novi Sad.[46] These tensions occasionally became public, eroding the Allies' fragile cohesion. Conversely, the unilateral way in which targets were selected left the US singularly vulnerable to international censure when mishaps occurred, such as the mistaken bombing of the Chinese Embassy in Belgrade on 5 May 1999.

The air campaign called for two simultaneous lines of attack: a strategic attack on Serb air defences and command-and-control facilities, the army and police and major supply routes, as well as refining sites for petroleum, oil and lubricants; and a theatre campaign in Kosovo against Serb forces there.[47] In reality, this was achieved only for about two weeks in the middle of the war, between the NATO summit in late April and the Chinese Embassy bombing, and in the last weeks leading up to the cease-fire on 10 June 1999.[48] While political constraints made it difficult to agree on fixed strategic targets, especially those near Belgrade, NATO was militarily unable to engage mobile targets in Kosovo effectively through air-power alone. The result was a protracted war which risked the dissolution of the coalition as it progressed. Yugoslavia's attempt to wait out the coalition in the hope that it would lose its resolve was therefore a logical course of action. At the outset of the war, this strategy stood a reasonable chance of success. The absence of dramatic results within the first week eroded public confidence, and individual NATO countries grew increasingly sceptical that air-power alone would force the withdrawal of Yugoslav forces from Kosovo. They thus began to float numerous uncoordinated alternatives, from Germany's suggestion of a pause in bombing to the UK's push for the introduction of ground forces.[49]

Multinational Doctrine

Whereas the Gulf War demonstrated the benefits of common doctrine and Bosnia showed the need to develop new operational concepts tailored to peacekeeping, Kosovo revealed the growing divergence between European war-fighting doctrines and emerging US concepts. These concepts share certain uniquely American characteristics, which are increasingly at odds with traditional NATO and European doctrines. America's Vietnam experience did much to discredit the theory of limited war, and the belief that the use of military force could be precisely calibrated according to an adversary's moves. Since the 1970s, the US officer corps has rejected graduated military campaigns in favour of the early and overwhelming use of force. Emerging concepts are also placing greater weight on minimising US casualties by attacking at stand-off range, suppressing enemy air defences, and defending against chemical and biological weapons, missiles and mines. The US is more willing than its major Allies to incorporate nascent technologies into its new concepts. Finally, since the mid-1980s the US has placed much greater emphasis on joint operations.

One promising US operational concept is Parallel Warfare, which calls for simultaneous attacks against an enemy's key systems so as to paralyse it.[50] Another similar concept is Rapid Dominance, the key objective of which is 'to impose [an] overwhelming level of shock and awe against an adversary on an immediate or sufficiently timely basis to paralyse its will to carry on'.[51] Concepts such as these exploit the US military's advantages in high technology and air-power, and would ideally be employed in operations that the US conducted alone. However, Kosovo demonstrated how difficult it is to apply them within a coalition. Most European militaries lack both the capabilities needed to implement these concepts, and the doctrinal inclination to undertake operations based on them. As one French commentator observed: 'Unlike the Americans, and with the exception of the British, the Europeans are avoiding speaking – at least, in public – of a devastating increase in power against Yugoslavia'.[52] During the Cold War, the threat of Soviet aggression demanded as much convergence between European and US doctrines as possible. Today, there is no such enforcing mechanism. Concepts like Parallel Warfare and Rapid Dominance are not driven by the requirements of the European theatre, but by those of the Persian Gulf, the Korean Peninsula and other distant regions. European militaries envisage different requirements for the types of operations closer to home that they anticipate undertaking.

Key Capabilities

The Kosovo campaign reinforced perceptions of a growing gap between the capabilities of the US and those of its European Allies. After the war, the French Ministry of Defence noted that:

> *There exists a great imbalance in favour of the Americans. Although Europe provided a sufficient number of aircraft, American advances amplified the effects of a technological gap. This situation allows the US to play a dominant role, notably in command structures.*[53]

Forging a more equitable partnership will mean addressing this imbalance, especially in four areas: strike support; intelligence, surveillance and reconnaissance; communications and command-and-control; and precision attack.

Strike Support

The Kosovo conflict confirmed the decisive role played by traditional enabling capabilities, such as aerial refuelling, airborne command-and-control, battle management, ground surveillance, electronic warfare and combat search and rescue. The US dominated in all of these areas: while non-US Allies conducted 47% of strike sorties, they flew only 29% of support sorties.[54] Every European strike sortie required an average of three US support aircraft to suppress enemy radar, refuel and direct the battle.[55] Where France contributed ten refuelling aircraft, the UK nine and Germany none, the US committed more than 150.[56] After the war, the French Ministry of Defence identified refuelling in particular as critical to maintaining the country's strategic autonomy.[57]

Air-traffic control posed immense problems for the NATO Combined Air Operations Centre (CAOC) in Vicenza, Italy, which coordinated and planned the air attacks. The intricately layered airspace, tight corridors of approach around Kosovo and deconfliction of civil and military aircraft across Europe made the conflict particularly challenging for air-traffic control. NATO aircraft operated from bases as far afield as Incirlik in Turkey and Lakenheath in the UK (B-2 bombers also operated out of the US, but were not directed by Allied air-traffic-control systems). Here again, there was insufficient consultation between the Allies before the campaign began, and inadequate coordination once it got under way. US B-2 and F-117 stealth aircraft, as well as some cruise-missile strikes and UAV sorties, were not included in the daily ATO.[58] US, British, French and NATO E-3 airborne warning and control system (AWACS) aircraft were indispensable in managing air traffic, but some pilots complained that they received poor flight guidance from NATO AWACS, which were optimised for early-warning, rather than airborne command-and-control and battle management.[59]

The air campaign also revealed a general shortage of radar-jamming and SEAD aircraft, as well as, for some Allies, anti-radar missiles. Throughout the 1990s, critical electronic-warfare capabilities, such as US EF-111 and F-4G aircraft, were retired. The emphasis on electronic warfare declined, both in NATO's tactical evaluations (TACEVALS) – the readiness inspections required for all Allied air force units – and in multinational exercises. This meant that the Allies were not adequately prepared for air operations against countries like Yugoslavia, with its dense integrated air defences.[60] The European Allies depended upon the US for electronic-warfare missions and the suppression of Yugoslav air defences, although the US, which provided 40 EA-6B *Prowlers* out of a total world-wide of 95, found its resources stretched.[61]

Combat search-and-rescue capabilities were also insufficient. Europeans were almost completely dependent on the US in this area;

of all the European countries involved, only France made a (modest) contribution.[62] Despite the emphasis in the West on minimising the number of casualties suffered or prisoners of war taken by the enemy, there is little appreciation of what combat search and rescue can entail. By early 2000, no unclassified figures had been made available regarding combat search and rescue in Kosovo, though earlier air operations over Bosnia indicate the immense effort involved. For example, 500 missions were flown in five days to bring out a US pilot, Captain Scott O'Grady, whose aircraft had been brought down over Bosnia in June 1995.[63] This was roughly equal to half of the total British strike sorties flown during the entire Kosovo conflict.[64]

Intelligence, Surveillance and Reconnaissance
The US met approximately 95% of NATO's intelligence require-ments.[65] However, the timely release of US intelligence to Allies proved difficult. According to an RAF study, location data and images of Yugoslav mobile targets took up to 72 hours to reach squadrons, making it impossible to attack them before they moved.[66] US military officials have conceded that the process by which intelligence is cleared for release is cumbersome and time-consuming.[67]

Some capabilities only the US could provide, including *Predator* UAVs, RC-135 *Rivet Joint* aircraft, U-2 reconnaissance planes, and JSTARS ground-surveillance aircraft, although these were in short supply. Only two JSTARS were in the theatre, and could not maintain continuous coverage over Yugoslavia throughout the campaign. Although France deployed its *Horizon* helicopter surveillance system to supplement JSTARS, it could not easily be integrated into the Allied surveillance architecture and was thus of little benefit.[68] Given the risks involved in their use, tactical manned reconnaissance aircraft (one area in which the European Allies have an advantage) were of less value than stand-off and unmanned vehicles, such as French and German CL-289 drones and US *Predators*.

Lessons from the conflict have challenged previous thinking, especially in Europe, about the relative importance of strategic intelligence provided by satellites, and intelligence provided by theatre-reconnaissance and surveillance manned aircraft and drones.

Both the UK and Germany are studying the feasibility of using drones as surrogates for satellites, as well as to designate and even destroy targets.[69] France is also reassessing the utility of satellite surveillance versus airborne systems. Following the conflict, French Defence Minister Richard noted that: 'The fact remains that satellites' role in battle is not crucial. They are too high up. It is better to use drones or reconnaissance aircraft, and of course human intelligence. We have not had the feeling that the United States has been very far in the lead in these fields'.[70] A French study in June 1999 noted how well the *Helios* reconnaissance satellite was complemented by the country's tactical reconnaissance aircraft, such as the *Mirage* F-1CR, *Super Etendard* IV PM and *Mirage* IV P, as well as by the *Horizon* system, which was used to locate mobile ground targets.[71] It concluded that, in addition to strategic intelligence provided by satellites, using these systems to acquire targets, locate enemy positions and assess battle damage was key to autonomous decision-making and the ability to plan and conduct operations.[72]

Communications, Command-and-Control and Information Networks

Kosovo highlighted both the central role that networked communications and information systems play in modern coalitions, and the operational difficulties and interoperability problems that new technologies can bring. The lack of secure communications was a particular issue. After the air campaign, US Secretary of Defense Cohen warned of 'some real gaps in secure communications with some of our allies'.[73] Although NATO had acquired 1,200 STU-IIB secure telephones prior to the conflict, only 72 were in the Southern Region, and the majority of these were already dedicated to operations in Bosnia. As with IFOR, they were not interoperable with the STU-IIIs brought in by US forces.[74] It was thus difficult for the Allies to pass secure voice messages and facsimiles among themselves. The major US and NATO secure-messaging systems (the US Secret Internet Protocol Network (SIPRNET) and NATO's CRONOS) were also not interoperable. Finally, the lack of secure, interoperable aircraft communications and anti-jam radios meant that command-and-control aircraft and other Allied planes had to pass information in the clear, thereby badly compromising operational security.[75]

As in Bosnia, the Kosovo operation relied heavily on Web-based technologies, e-mail and video-conferencing. Again, common secure systems were lacking, and there were difficulties in transmitting high volumes of information within a restricted amount of bandwidth. Peacetime procedures for managing the use of these new technologies in conflict were also inadequate. Difficulties emerged between the Allies in sharing bandwidth, linking disparate information systems, establishing common standards for network security and passing on time-sensitive intelligence.[76] The fact that US and NATO intelligence networks were not interoperable, together with the use of different classification standards, only exacerbated these problems.[77]

Perhaps the most glaring weakness of all the major Allies, including the US, was in secure and rapid aircraft data-links. Although Allied tactical-reconnaissance and ground-surveillance aircraft and drones provided high-resolution imagery for the CAOC, they could not pass this information directly to strike aircraft in the region, which did not have the necessary data-links. Nor could the CAOC quickly disseminate this information to attack squadrons. Consequently, it normally took three to four hours for intelligence from surveillance aircraft to reach strike aircraft.[78] In addition, although many US and British combat aircraft had JTIDS/Link 16 data-links and *Have Quick* secure radios, they were forced to use non-secure systems to communicate with other major Allies which did not have this equipment.[79] Thus, the coalition squandered many of the benefits of advanced surveillance and precision strike. A group of Allies, including the US, France and Germany, is developing the MIDS common data-link, which will be interoperable with JTIDS/Link 16. MIDS should speed up the transfer of targeting information to attack aircraft.

Precision Attack

The Kosovo conflict revealed that, although the Europeans had enough combat aircraft, they suffered from severe shortages of precision munitions. With the exception of the UK's *Tomahawk* cruise missiles, 21 of which were fired during the campaign, only the US had all-weather aircraft and munitions capable of conducting attacks through heavy cloud cover.[80] Poor weather conditions coupled with the need to minimise collateral damage meant that the US carried out a disproportionate number of attacks in the critical early days of the war.[81] Had the US suffered significant casualties, or had the level of collateral damage been much higher, the effects on coalition cohesion could have been devastating. Conversely, European countries that did not have cruise missiles, such as France, were denied a say in how they were used. In its after-action report, the French Ministry of Defence concluded that the 'use of [cruise missiles] by American and British forces emphasised the inescapable centralised planning process. It thus appears that nations equipped with cruise missiles retain control over their use while, on the contrary, nations without them may find themselves excluded from those aspects of the decision-making cycle relating to strikes'.[82]

Both the US and its European Allies have a stake in ensuring that the risks and responsibilities of attacks are equitably shared. As with nuclear roles within NATO, the participation of as many Allies as possible in the planning and execution of conventional attacks would strengthen both the political and military cohesion of coalitions during crises. The more controversial the mission, the less inclined the US will be to undertake it alone on behalf of a wider coalition. As a senior American official put it:

> *It's in the political interest of the coalition to have all the allies militarily active. It's hard if [all the Allies] don't have the weapons in hand. We saw a lot of requests for GBUs [glide-bomb units], JDAMs [Joint Direct Attack Munitions], Mavericks and LANTIRN [infrared targeting] pods because our Allies realized the rules of engagement required precision.*[83]

European states need further to develop the capabilities for effective attack operations if they are to have a greater voice in how these operations are conducted. France plans to introduce new long-range air-to-ground missiles, including the *Apache* runway-attack missile in 2001 and the SCALP EG long-range cruise missile in 2003.[84] The SCALP is designed to use the global positioning system (GPS) for mid-course updates in addition to terrain navigation and inertial guidance. The UK's introduction of the *Storm Shadow* (the British equivalent of the SCALP), as well as *Brimstone* air-to-ground anti-armour missiles for *Harrier* GR-7 and *Eurofighter* aircraft, will partially rectify its shortfalls in precision munitions.[85] Germany plans to acquire the *Taurus* stand-off, precision-guided cruise missile.[86] The major European Allies, especially France, are also improving their night-vision capabilities. Whereas no French aircraft had night-vision equipment in the Gulf, eight *Mirage* 2000Ds regularly flew night missions during the Kosovo conflict. However, thermal camera laser-designation pods (which allow pilots to 'tag' targets with a laser beam) were available for only a quarter of the country's *Mirage* 2000Ds, and older *Jaguars*, *Mirage* F1 CTs and *Super Etendards* were not equipped with them.[87]

For the main European countries, one potential obstacle to the rapid procurement of additional night-vision capabilities and stand-off precision munitions is that the major Allies remain locked into acquiring large new fleets of combat aircraft – the *Eurofighter*, *Rafale* and the US Joint Strike Fighter. There is a danger that aircraft procurement will crowd out increased investment in the advanced munitions, target-acquisition systems and data-links needed for rapid precision attacks. To be able to conduct precision strikes without the US, Europeans will require both aerial and space-based sensors, the full range of strike-support capabilities, including wide-area ground-surveillance aircraft, data-links, and all-weather platforms and munitions. These capabilities are likely to remain beyond the reach of any individual European country for at least a decade.

The Lessons of the 1990s

The operations in the Gulf, Bosnia and Kosovo all demonstrated the difficulties involved in forming coalitions and undertaking multinational action. They revealed the widening gap between the capabilities of the US, and those of its European Allies; the increasing inapplicability of NATO's Cold War war-fighting doctrine to operations like Bosnia and Kosovo; the growing divergence between European doctrines and emerging US concepts; and the Allies' collective failure to prepare adequately for coalitions.

Capability problems are particularly acute in five key areas: strike support; precision attack; strategic transport; force protection; and communications. The Gulf War and Kosovo demonstrated the gulf between US and European capacities to support strike operations with refuelling aircraft, and UAVs or manned aircraft to conduct surveillance and reconnaissance missions, and jam or destroy enemy air-defence systems. European forces depend upon the US to conduct the vast majority of stand-off, precision ground attacks in all weather conditions. European transport capabilities are also inadequate. Although the emphasis has been on acquiring large aircraft akin to the US C-17, sealift is arguably more important for the envisaged European reaction force of 50,000–60,000 troops. Although slower than aircraft, roll-on, roll-off ships are a cheaper way of transporting heavy brigades to crisis spots. Greater attention also needs to be paid to ensuring the survivability of forces and their capacity to operate in adverse conditions. In addition to stand-off munitions, this means defences against NBC weapons and ballistic and cruise missiles, transmitters to identify allies and enemies, electronic countermeasures, and improved search-and-rescue capacities. Finally, increasingly complex military operations need interoperable, high-speed, high-volume secure communications, including data-links. All of the Allies, including the US, have underinvested in the latter area.

There are also growing differences between the Allies in terms of doctrine and operational concepts. While NATO doctrine was applicable in the Gulf War, it has had much less salience in the smaller crisis-response operations in the Balkans. As a result, the Allies were forced to operate in an *ad hoc*, trial-and-error way. Moreover, whereas the US has begun to adopt concepts such as Parallel Warfare and Rapid Dominance, European countries, particularly the UK and France, have focused more on adapting their doctrines to meet the challenges of peace-support operations. For the US, such missions are part of a broader, more generic category of 'operations other than war', which is better at explaining what it is not, than at explaining what it is. The different weights that countries place on major doctrinal principles like protection, surprise and initiative compound the difficulties in crafting common operational plans.

Lastly, the transatlantic Allies have collectively failed to prepare adequately for coalition operations. Firm political guidance on what threat scenarios to consider, as well as combined pre-crisis planning, coordination and consultation on strategy and targets, have all been lacking. Many of the tensions that emerged during the Kosovo conflict were the direct result of insufficient effort to reconcile competing national approaches to operations in the months running up to the start of air strikes. Attempts to do so during the conflict only increased tensions within the coalition, and provided Belgrade with a chance to split it. Addressing all of these issues at once is unlikely to succeed in resolving them.

Chapter 3

Preparing for Future Operations

Improving the performance of future coalitions will require a much greater emphasis on combined force planning in peace. To achieve this, the transatlantic Allies will have to address three critical issues: the impact of a revolution in military affairs (RMA); the roles of NATO and the EU in defence planning, as well as non-institutional approaches; and the need for greater role specialisation. The Gulf War suggested that new technologies have wrought revolutionary changes in how war is waged. If some form of transformation is indeed under way, the transatlantic Allies will need to modify how they prepare for coalitions. Second, Kosovo demonstrated the limits of the formal NATO Alliance and underscored the fact that Europe must improve its defence capabilities. It also highlighted the need for the core Allies to adopt non-institutional approaches to improve their capabilities and harmonise their concepts and plans. Finally, operations in the 1990s made clear that, if future coalitions are to be more effective and efficient, the transatlantic Allies will have to adopt some form of role specialisation. No Ally, not even the US, will remain capable of performing alone all the tasks required by modern military missions.

The Impact of a Revolution in Military Affairs

Since the mid-1980s, defence analysts and scholars have debated whether an RMA has begun. The US Department of Defense Office of Net Assessment defines an RMA as 'a major change in the nature of warfare brought about by the innovative application of technologies which, combined with dramatic changes in military doctrine and operational concepts, fundamentally alters the character and conduct of operations'.[1] Unlike previous RMAs that centred on the introduction of new weapons or platforms, today's posited 'revolution' has less to do with specific new technologies than with the complex way in which they are integrated, forming what US Admiral William Owens has described as a 'system of systems', which links advanced surveillance sensors with data-processing and communications networks, as well as precision-attack platforms and munitions.[2]

Such integration suggests that decision-making will be dramatically accelerated as information is transferred from sensors to strike forces more rapidly. This raises questions about how much influence countries can have over decisions made in minutes, rather than hours. Missile defence illustrates the dilemma countries may face in the future between maintaining political control over their national forces, and responding rapidly to operational problems. As General Klaus Naumann has put it:

> *Are nations willing to permanently relinquish a degree of their sovereignty to enable a virtually automatic theatre missile defence system to engage an inbound missile knowing that sensors in one nation may trigger the launch of weapons in another nation with an anticipated interception above a third nation all within the space of a few seconds?*[3]

In future coalitions, forces and capabilities will be integrated at a lower level of command, but at a higher level of complexity. Decisions will be made almost instantly, operations will be spread over larger areas, and command authority will be far more decentralised. Consequently, it will be increasingly difficult for political leaders to exercise timely and effective control over the use of their national forces. Reconciling political control with the need to accelerate operational decision-making will demand greater consultation in peacetime.

The US and its major European Allies agree about the types of capabilities that will probably matter most in future conflicts; all have, for example, emphasised the importance of networked information and communications systems, better sensors and precision weapons.[4] But they have profoundly different views about what an RMA would mean for coalitions. If they adopt radically different approaches to reshaping their military forces, current disparities in capabilities and doctrines may widen. There are three major concerns about the potential impact of an RMA on coalitions in the future: affordability; changes in the transatlantic political balance; and the applicability of RMA-related forces and capabilities to operations other than major high-intensity conflicts.

Affordability

There is concern in Europe that an RMA-driven spending gap may drive a wedge between US and European militaries, increasing the imbalance in military capabilities. As Admiral Sir Jock Slater, a former British First Sea Lord, put it in 1998: 'The money the US is now spending on digitisation is such that they could get out of step with their allies'.[5] Budgetary constraints have become the prism through which many European defence ministries evaluate the RMA. Germany typifies this prevailing attitude. Analysts Robbin Laird and Holger Mey argue that:

> the question of affordability dominates the discussion of the RMA in Germany. There is an inherent tension for the Germans between the need to maintain basic military capabilities (and thus the need to modernize across the board) and investing in new high-technology capabilities. Hence, the Germans will not put all their money into unproven concepts and high-tech weaponry for highly specialized tasks, but rather into those high-tech systems that promise to improve general capabilities.[6]

Concerns about affordability have led most European defence ministries to adopt an incremental approach to military innovation, focusing on using new technologies to improve existing capabilities, rather than designing radically different ones. However, overlaying advanced systems on current force structures, rather than fundamentally reforming militaries so as to reap the full benefits of new technologies, risks reinforcing the status quo, and making militaries less adaptable. It could also discourage the adoption of new concepts and organisational structures.

In the absence of a clear, common and compelling threat, many European governments question whether there is an urgent need to accelerate technological and conceptual innovation. Rather, they argue, the US should temper its enthusiasm for new and sophisticated equipment, and instead concentrate on preserving interoperability with its key partners. Conversely, there is a growing sense in the US that incompatibility may be inevitable because Europeans will not keep up with the pace of change. A bipartisan US Commission study in September 1999, for example, concluded that: 'the United States will increasingly find itself wishing to form coalitions but increasingly unable to find partners willing and able to carry out combined military operations'.[7] Paradoxically, predictions of an inevitable and unbridgeable gap between the US and its Allies have reinforced the strong inclination within the US military to ensure that it retains the capacity for unilateral action.

However, neither incompatibility nor a widening of the gap between the capabilities of the transatlantic Allies is inevitable. As US analyst Andrew Krepinevich has observed:

> *A military revolution now underway promises to change traditional (nonnuclear) warfare on a scale not seen since the period between the two world wars. Typically such revolutions produce a substantial decline in the value of certain defense systems. The United States, with by far the world's largest inventory of military capital stock, stands to lose most from this phenomenon.*[8]

Conversely, the European Allies may benefit relatively more than the US from an RMA. Europe's smaller militaries and relatively fewer 'sunk costs' in status-quo systems and technologies could allow European armed forces greater agility in adopting promising new technologies and concepts. Driven largely by commercial information technologies, an RMA would benefit all countries with highly educated militaries and doctrines that encourage decentralised decision-making by independent, lower-level commanders. Finally, since the European Allies do not have the global security responsibilities of the US and face no immediate threat, there is less incentive for them to maintain their increasingly out-dated military systems and concepts.

Changes in the Transatlantic Balance

Many French analysts have voiced concerns about whether countries such as their own can maintain their strategic independence and capacity for autonomous decision-making in an era of military change dominated by the US. Pierre Fiorini, for example, has warned that 'National sovereignty is at stake in the mastery of systems for the acquisition and processing of information. These systems in fact constitute the infrastructures that provide the basis on which decision-making takes place at every level'.[9] There is also concern that Europe's dependence on the US for intelligence, combined with the pace of operations and the degree to which forces need to be integrated, might bind Europe too closely to the US strategically. Yves Boyer, for instance, has argued that the US could exploit an RMA to dominate its European Allies by centralising decision-making and consolidating its monopoly over intelligence and command-and-control capabilities.[10]

However, these arguments overstate the political risks of integration, and understate its considerable operational benefits. They ignore the fundamental characteristic of a contemporary RMA: the complex integration of disparate and widely dispersed systems.[11] This does not require adopting *common* systems; on the contrary, emerging technologies offer the possibility of linking together different types of national command-and-control systems via standardised interfaces.[12] Advances in commercial off-the-shelf technologies (COTs) will also help to ensure that no one nation dominates future command-and-control arrangements, because most technology will originate in the commercial world and will, therefore, be equally available to all. The growing dominance of COTs also implies that, in time, the gap between US and European spending on research and development (R&D) may not matter as much, since R&D is being driven increasingly by private, rather than public, investment.

Applicability

For the foreseeable future, the US and its European Allies are most likely to face smaller-scale contingencies, rather than major conflict. How relevant would an RMA be in these types of operations? Lawrence Freedman has argued that the proliferation of weak states and prolonged internal conflict will have a greater impact on how military operations are conducted than the US version of an RMA, with its focus on high-technology, high-intensity war.[13] Europe's more traditional, labour-intensive forces would, Freedman argues, actually be better at dealing with these types of situation than US 'RMA-type' forces, since technology cannot substitute for soldiers on the ground in peace-support and constabulary missions.[14]

There is no doubt that human beings will remain vital in any military operation. Nevertheless, coalition commanders will want many of the high-technology systems and forces associated with an RMA, even for non-combat operations such as peacekeeping. Technologies and concepts related to an RMA could make such operations more effective in a number of ways. Remote sensing could make peacekeeping easier by allowing the separation of opposing parties to be monitored at minimal risk to coalition forces. Precision force could make it easier for coalition commanders to control the level and scope of violence.[15] This, combined with better surveillance systems, could enable new stand-off approaches to peace-support operations, whereby technologically superior, albeit smaller, forces control a wider geographic area.[16] Finally, non-lethal weapons would lower the threshold for using force in constabulary missions, reduce collateral damage, and help to control the escalation of violence.[17]

Harmonising National Approaches

The RMA entails political and military risks for the transatlantic Allies. For the US, transforming its forces while still being able to build effective coalitions will require modifying its blueprint for change. *Joint Vision 2010*, the template by which US military forces are to exploit new information, communications and guidance technologies, acknowledges that nearly all future US operations will be conducted as part of a coalition, but its discussion of the implications of this assumption is insufficient.[18] Instead, it focuses on attaining 'decisive unilateral strength' so as to fight and win wars alone, if necessary.[19] Striking a better balance between unilateral and multilateral capabilities will be critical to reconciling revolutionary technologies and innovative concepts with the need to form coalitions. This will mean taking greater risks in the short term by relying more on coalition partners so that the US can reallocate effort and resources to addressing more menacing longer-term threats. By contrast, Europeans risk missing out on the opportunities that an RMA offers. Embracing it and embarking on a programme of radical change may be the only way for European militaries to reduce the disparity between US capabilities and their own, and achieve true defence autonomy. Adopting advanced technologies (such as precision-guided munitions, unmanned surveillance systems, missile defences and high-speed information and communications networks), as well as new operational concepts to exploit them, would help all the Allies to meet the challenges that they have faced since the end of the Cold War: minimising casualties and collateral damage, projecting power rapidly and integrating their forces smoothly into coalitions.

Frameworks for Defence Planning

The second issue confronting the transatlantic Allies concerns the institutional arrangements for planning and conducting coalition operations. NATO has shown itself to be an effective multinational arrangement for coordinating the Allies' defence plans, deterring large-scale invasion and conducting peace-support operations like IFOR. But the Alliance may not be the best framework for planning or carrying out expeditionary combat missions. Kosovo showed the limitations of conducting an offensive combat operation within a 19-member alliance whose primary purpose is defensive. Although the objectives were met, NATO's procedures were too inflexible, while the need to maintain cohesion drove operations towards the lowest common denominator of political will and military effort. Above all, the Alliance's complex decision-making process and procedures for political consultation made it more difficult for NATO forces to take the initiative and maintain the tempo of attacks.

As an alternative to operations commanded by NATO, *ad hoc* coalitions of those Allies most willing and able to use force in large-scale combat operations may be preferable. As Richard Haass has argued:

> *What is needed is an inherently flexible approach to foreign policy that can respond to unforeseen situations in unprecedented ways.* [Ad hoc] *coalitions bring with them some of*

> *the advantages that derive from collective effort (resources, specialization, etc.) without the need for consensus or prearranged authority.*[20]

As operational decisions are taken more quickly, political decision-making will need to be just as responsive to exploit the Allies' military advantage of speed. This points to smaller, more cohesive coalitions, with a single, simple command structure more akin to the Gulf War's than Kosovo's. NATO may thus choose to endorse politically the military actions of a subset of its members under-taking an operation in the general interests of the whole.[21] The US and its major European Allies should also exploit their potential to reform their militaries faster than NATO as a whole, by placing greater emphasis on non-institutional preparation in peacetime. *Ad hoc* coalitions formed in a crisis demand greater *ad hoc* preparations in peacetime.

NATO's Changing Role

Rather than acting as a regional *gendarme* or the default framework for US–European military operations in all cases, NATO's greatest institutional contribution will be as the key facilitator and training ground for coalitions formed either within, or outside of, the Alliance framework.

The Alliance has taken important steps to enhance its role as a coalition facilitator, most notably by developing the Combined Joint Task Force (CJTF) concept, under which subsets of NATO members may form coalitions, while drawing on Alliance headquarters and assets. At the same time, the Alliance has reinforced its capacity for collective defence. The distinction between Article 5 and non-Article 5 capabilities – that is, between collective defence and crisis response – has become artificial. Modern collective defence and out-of-area crisis response share the same vital requirement: projecting combat forces rapidly over great distances. In the wake of its enlargement, the ability to project forces to the Vistula or the Euphrates is as relevant to NATO's credibility as a collective-defence organisation as was defending West Germany at the Elbe during the Cold War. There is thus an obligation on NATO members, especially those which are no longer front-line states, to build capabilities so as to come rapidly to the defence of their most vulnerable Allies. Doing so would also make the Allies better able to conduct expeditionary operations beyond Europe.

During the Kosovo air operation in April 1999, NATO heads of state and government unveiled a new Strategic Concept designed to improve force-projection capabilities, both for collective defence and for crisis response. Alliance members agreed to 'contribute to effective conflict prevention and to engage actively in crisis management, including crisis response operations'.[22] The Alliance is also playing an important role in harmonising national perspectives on future threats and changes in the nature of warfare. The NATO Senior Defence Group on Proliferation and the Conference of National Armaments Directors are acting as a catalyst for Allied efforts to develop ways to counter unconventional threats, such as chemical and biological weapons and ballistic missiles. The US-proposed DCI, endorsed by NATO in April 1999, addresses the most prominent shortfalls revealed by coalition operations in the 1990s, and promotes Allied cooperation in concept development and experimentation.[23] Through the DCI, the Allies are also coordinating their views on future military operations. NATO has tasked the Supreme Allied Commander Atlantic (SACLANT), Admiral Harold Gehman, to devise a programme for the cooperative development of new operational concepts.[24] Developing such common concepts would be the first step towards revising NATO's out-dated doctrine so as to meet new security challenges.

NATO is also a suitable framework for making communications and information systems interoperable. By 2002, the Alliance plans to develop a common communications, command and control architecture to which individual members can link their national systems. This will in turn provide a basis for refining interoperability standards. In particular, NATO will focus on four areas: digitisation, deployability, security and the management of military access to the radio-frequency spectrum.[25] NATO standards will be the default ones for any Western coalition, while its command-and-control structure will help in forming and managing *ad hoc* coalitions involving only some of the Allies.

All of these steps will help to improve the performance of future US–European coalitions. However, on its own, NATO is unlikely to spur European states to increase defence spending, remove all of the discrepancies in capabilities revealed by operations in the 1990s, or convince reluctant militaries radically to reshape their forces. Nor will changes in NATO have much effect on US programmes, or on the United States' global posture. The DCI and related efforts will have greatest impact in improving the capabilities of the weakest Allies. Improving the capabilities and forces of the core transatlantic Allies will, however, require additional, complementary efforts and coordination outside of NATO. As a result, the major European Allies are working through the EU to correct the deficiencies in their capabilities.

The EU's Emerging Role

The EU is becoming more assertive in security policy, and in its aspirations for an autonomous defence capability. At their June 1999 summit in Cologne, European leaders pledged their support for improving Europe's collective military capabilities to address regional security challenges. Lessons from Kosovo loom large; as George Robertson put it: 'In Kosovo, we have all come face to face with the European future, and it is frightening'.[26] Kosovo may become for Europe what Grenada was for the US. In the wake of the successful, although flawed, invasion of the island in 1983, the US introduced reforms to improve coordination between the services and streamline command-and-control structures. Similarly, Kosovo may prompt the European Allies to increase their coordination, interoperability and force-projection capabilities, thereby allowing more balanced contributions to future coalition operations.

Since the 1970s, the US, working through NATO, has largely failed to persuade European countries to increase their defence spending. If change is to occur, the impetus must come from within. The EU could be essential in pushing its members to step up their expenditure and to develop the requisite capabilities for future coalition operations.

EU members have committed themselves to a 'Headline Goal' of fielding troops for a rapidly deployable and sustainable corps of between 50,000 and 60,000 personnel by 2003. They have also agreed 'Collective Capability Goals' for improving command and control, intelligence and strategic transport.[27] To meet these objectives, EU members are preparing to establish a European air-transport command, and are enhancing their sealift capacity. These efforts focus on the capabilities needed to perform the kinds of tasks outlined in the EU's Petersberg Declaration of 1992. These range from humanitarian and rescue missions, through peacekeeping to combat crisis-management and 'peacemaking' missions.[28] The Petersberg Declaration placed no geographical limits on the tasks to be undertaken. If contingencies beyond Western Europe are envisaged, then the EU's goals could substantially rebalance US and European capacities. Developing the power-projection capabilities needed for operations outside of Western Europe could, moreover, prompt a change in strategic outlook among EU states, leading them to think more in terms of broader European interests that are affected on a global basis, rather than the narrower regional interests of individual countries. Meeting the requirements of the most difficult Petersberg tasks would also furnish many of the capabilities needed to participate alongside US forces in large-scale combat operations in, or beyond, Europe. This would help to reconcile the EU's Headline and Capability Goals with NATO's DCI objectives of improved deployability, logistics, strike assets, force protection and communications, command and control. On the other hand, if EU states choose more modest scenarios that emphasise threats closer to home and only at the lower end of the Petersberg spectrum, this is more likely to justify the continued slide in their defence budgets, making transatlantic imbalances more enduring.

Barring an EU-driven rearmament blueprint akin to US National Security Council Memorandum 68 of 1950, which trebled the US defence budget, it is unlikely that the European Allies will, in the foreseeable future, be able to close all of their capability gaps *vis-à-vis* the US. The EU is unlikely to achieve a truly autonomous defence capability in the next 10–15 years which would allow it to carry out medium-sized combat operations such as Kosovo without the US. Paradoxically, acknowledging this could lead EU states to accept a greater degree of dependence on the US as a coalition partner in the short term, so as to achieve real military autonomy in the long term. By accepting their reliance on the US in areas where it has a preponderant lead – such as strategic intelligence and air-power – European states could adopt a more radical approach to an RMA. They could choose to cancel costly modernisation programmes, such as upgrades for their fleets of tanks and combat aircraft, in favour of acquiring advanced systems such as data-links, cruise missiles, GPS-guided bombs, UAVs, missile defences and strategic transport ships and aircraft. This would help to close the qualitative gap with the US, and thereby ensure Europe a greater voice in future transatlantic coalitions. From an American perspective, increased European investment in advanced military systems would offer greater potential for sharing more equitably the risks and responsibilities of future operations.

Non-Institutional Approaches

NATO and the EU will be essential in raising the equipment and force standards of their members. However, there are several areas in which closer, non-institutional cooperation between the major Allies would improve their performance in future coalition operations. Attempts should be made to harmonise the strategic outlooks of the major Allies, taking better account of potential Allied contributions to operations, and enhancing their doctrinal and organisational understanding.

As a foundation for other non-institutional efforts, peacetime intelligence-sharing between the major Allies should be improved. Assessments of military threats will drive operational planning, serve as the basis for exercises and training, inform the development of doctrine and provide a yardstick for force planning. Moreover, achieving a common operational picture in a crisis will require practising the routine exchange of information in peacetime. Coalitions in the 1990s demonstrated the strategic and operational difficulties caused by cumbersome release procedures. Standing procedures must be developed to ensure the timely release of information in a crisis. The Allies also need to cooperate in developing threat assessments on critical regions outside of Europe, especially in the Middle East and North Africa. While NATO prepares a common intelligence estimate (MC 161) each year, this is subject to the approval of all 19 Allies, and countries must consider what intelligence they are willing to share with the Alliance as a whole; as a result, security concerns and political sensitivities have tended to soften the edges of NATO's assessments. Undertaking threat assessments among the major Allies in peacetime would encourage them to harmonise their strategic outlooks. Such assessments would also reduce the need for individual countries to acquire their own national, and duplicative, intelligence systems.

Coalition operations in the 1990s also revealed the pitfalls of unilateral operational planning, particularly by the US. Outside of Europe, US military commanders do not coordinate contingency plans with the major European Allies. There is a need for consultation between the US and key European militaries about the objectives of a given plan, target sets, rules of engagement and logistical requirements. European countries would also benefit from being given an insight into US planning. They would have the opportunity to make their concerns known in peacetime, thereby ensuring that coalitions are formed smoothly in a crisis.

Similarly, the major Allies would benefit from expanding and intensifying exercises and manoeuvres conducted outside the context of NATO. Political constraints prevent the Alliance from conducting certain types of exercises that could be misinterpreted by Russia and other countries. For this reason, NATO no longer conducts the *Reforger* exercise series, although experience gained from it was instrumental in the success of the Gulf War coalition. Unlike NATO as a whole, the major Allies are more likely to contemplate deployments outside of Europe. Even Germany has shown an interest in extra-regional exercises, having participated in the US-led *Roving Sands*, which emphasised desert-warfare training for contingencies in the Middle East. There is a need for more cross-regional training through exercises such as the US-led *Bright Star*, involving North American, European and Middle Eastern countries, and aimed at countering threats outside of NATO's sphere.[29] As missile defence becomes increasingly important for all of the major Allies, interoperability trials and command-and-control exercises, such as the *Optic Windmill* series, would assist in attempts to harmonise Allied operational outlooks, and in agreeing rules of engagement so that operational decisions in a crisis can be made almost automatically.

Greater coordination of national doctrine and the development of operational concepts is another important area for greater *ad hoc* preparation. The political premise that most operations will, in the future, be conducted within coalitions should be translated into meaningful doctrine and operational concepts. This is especially true for the US. No matter how brilliant an operational concept is, if it fails to take account of the multinational context in which most future missions will be conducted, it risks failure. New operational concepts must be developed with an eye towards their application within coalitions. In time, solely national doctrine should become the exception, rather than the rule.

Towards Limited Role Specialisation

The final issue that the transatlantic Allies will have to address is how risks and responsibilities within a coalition will be shared, and how improvements to military capabilities will be prioritised. Budgetary and political constraints argue for some form of role specialisation, which might alleviate the need for identical, across-the-board improvements by every country. It could also make national contributions to coalitions more effective and reliable, thereby strengthening, rather than weakening, strategic unity between the Allies.

Both US and European planners oppose role specialisation within NATO, despite five decades of it happening implicitly: the US providing nuclear weapons, a blue-water navy and a large strategic bomber force for power projection, while the Europeans concentrated on fielding large ground forces to defend their borders, navies to patrol their coasts and air forces to defend their airspace. The US has opposed a division of labour between countries that conduct large-scale combat operations on the one hand, and countries that conduct peacekeeping missions on the other. The problem with such proposals, David Gompert and others have warned, is that they 'would run afoul of one of the most important and fundamental principles on which the cohesion of the Atlantic Alliance depends: the indivisibility of risk'.[30]

Role specialisation is also unattractive to Europeans, who fear that the US will leave messy ground wars to them in favour of low-risk air-power. A principal British concern is that role specialisation may prompt the US to reduce its relatively high-technology forces to the point where they can no longer carry out more labour-intensive peace-support operations.[31] Out of necessity, the US would then seek a new bargain whereby it provides intelligence capabilities and air-power, while its technologically inferior Allies take on more dangerous tasks on the ground.[32] This would be politically unacceptable to all the core Allies.

Given the opposition to role specialisation, proposals to harmonise the different rates of Allied reform and modernisation have tended to focus on across-the-board improvements in both capabilities and concepts. This approach is essential if all 19 NATO members are to share a common minimal level. However, it is the core transatlantic Allies that will, for the foreseeable future, make the most substantial contributions to coalitions. Since rates of change between them will differ, the key will be to prioritise better the improvements in capabilities being undertaken by each country, while ensuring that the force planning of the core Allies is complementary and coordinated. They should thus explore the possibility of limited role specialisation. Although they cannot with any certainty predict the contingencies that they will face, the Allies can anticipate the roles that they would be most willing to play, and the phases of an operation for which they would be best suited. If their roles and contributions were more predictable, Allies would probably become more reliable coalition partners.

To succeed, role specialisation must overcome the criticisms outlined above. It must avoid bifurcating collective-defence and peace-support responsibilities by recognising that all countries must maintain and improve their capacity for high-intensity combat. Such a proposal must ensure that mortal and material risks are equitably shared between coalition partners. Role specialisation should avoid a simple division between the US and Europe in favour of a more nuanced approach which recognises the importance of sharing risks and responsibilities in every facet of a coalition operation. It must demand a minimal level of participation by all parties in all phases of an operation. Role specialisation should be based on the unique political and military advantages and inclinations of each individual Ally. Finally, it should take account of new possibilities for coalition integration.

In the past, coalition forces have been integrated along geographic lines. The 1944 D-Day invasion of Normandy is a classic example, with sections of beach assigned to British, Canadian and American forces. The Gulf War and IFOR in Bosnia also followed this model: each country contributed forces, which were placed under the control of one nation's commander, but had relative autonomy within a geographic sector of the battlefield. The geographical, or spatial, integration of coalitions ensured command and control along national lines, and helped to avoid the fratricide that might have ensued in the absence of a clear delineation of national zones. However, it also assumed that all countries were willing to perform the tasks required in all phases of an operation. Thus, if a country was unwilling to participate in one phase of an operation, it had little choice but to forego participation in the operation as a whole.

The Kosovo operation and the political and military inclinations of the core Allies suggest that they are gradually shifting towards a new type of coalition integration that is more temporal than spatial.[33] In the Kosovo conflict, the US carried out the lion's share of the operation's air-combat phase, but has played a smaller role in the operation following the withdrawal of Yugoslav forces. On the other hand, the European Allies provided around 85% of KFOR's personnel following the end of the air campaign, and have shown themselves more willing than the US to shoulder the burdens of long-term peace-support operations in the Balkans. European militaries are relatively more manpower-intensive, and have a greater doctrinal inclination to undertake peacekeeping responsibilities. KFOR's command has rotated among British, German and Spanish general officers, suggesting the operation's increasing 'Europeanisation' in its last phase. More broadly, it implies that new divisions of labour are emerging among the Allies, with some focusing on the combat phase of an operation – both air and surface combat – and others on maintaining peace when hostilities end.

Current planning, especially in the US, rests largely on the principle of self-reliance. Each country maintains a full range of capabilities for high- and low-intensity tasks because it cannot necessarily depend on its Allies. Accepting limited role specialisation and coordinating the temporal integration of coalitions would allow each of the core Allies to narrow down their national planning priorities, while continuing to meet NATO's minimal requirements for combat capabilities. Countries could build forces and frame modernisation programmes to exploit their comparative advantages. Those better at spearheading the combat phase of a coalition operation, for example, would place greatest emphasis on air-power and special forces, air-mobile ground forces, information operations, stand-off/precision strike, target acquisition, rapid strategic transport by air and aerial-refuelling capabilities. Countries with a comparative advantage in conducting peace-support operations would require larger pools of deployable personnel to sustain regular force rotations; specialists such as linguists, engineers, mine-clearers, military police, and civil-affairs and medical personnel; higher-capacity sealift rather than faster airlift; and heavier forces and equipment to prevent any escalation of violence or renewal of war.

The US clearly prefers to spearhead high-intensity offensive operations, and is more reluctant than its European partners to engage in long-term peace-support operations. As Secretary of Defense Cohen put it in mid-1999: 'Peacekeeping is not [our] primary mission. Peacekeeping involves a different type of training and capabilities. There has been some gap in ... the training for the peacekeeping mission which is not necessarily consistent with the war-fighting mission we've had in the past'.[34] The US will increasingly avoid protracted deployments where its vital strategic interests are not directly at stake, in favour of maintaining its capacity for major combat.

Limited role specialisation would allow the US to reallocate resources to counter longer-term potential threats, while also honing its core competencies in long-range precision strike, rapid force projection and global surveillance and reconnaissance. Investment could focus on the capabilities needed for rapid deployment, offensive combat operations and force protection, to halt an invasion, establish a presence in a peace-support operation or beat an adversary in a regional conflict. At the same time, the US could reduce its investment in those capabilities needed to sustain peace-support operations, and would plan to withdraw the bulk of its forces shortly after the objectives of a combat operation had been met. Other Allies would provide the US with its 'exit strategy' by taking over once an adversary had been subdued and a peace-support operation was well-established. Under such a scheme, the US would be more inclined to commit forces to a coalition, since a prolonged engagement would be less likely, but it would also have to depend more on its coalition partners for the comprehensive management of conflicts.

At the other end of the spectrum, Germany avoided major participation in the combat portions of operations in the 1990s. Its contribution to the Kosovo campaign – 14 *Tornados* – was the smallest of any of the major Allies, while its opposition to a ground invasion was the strongest. Conversely, Germany has been willing to participate in peacekeeping operations, and has made one of the largest contributions of the major Allies to KFOR. The assumption of KFOR command by a German general in late 1999 demonstrated Germany's growing inclination to play a leading role in the peacekeeping operation, in contrast with its limited involvement in the preceding air campaign.

For Germany, limited role specialisation must not compromise the core capability to meet any resurgent threat to the country's territory. While the *Bundeswehr* is likely to become more professional and lighter, it will not give up the capacity to reconstitute a large armoured defence force. Nevertheless, it has a clear interest in demonstrating its relevance in the current security environment, above all by playing a greater role in crisis-management and peace-keeping. Moreover, many of the capabilities needed for territorial defence will also be applicable to peacekeeping. [For example, peacekeeping missions will also call for a force large and heavy enough to protect itself, control the escalation of violence and sustain and replenish itself during an operation that could last for several years. Force protection, tactical reconnaissance and ground surveil-lance, specialist units, heavy armour and transport ships, rather than high-speed transport aircraft, will also be planning priorities] To meet the additional requirements of peacekeeping, Germany would give greater priority in its armaments planning to developing non-lethal technologies, as well as UAVs and unattended ground sensors to monitor cease-fires. Above all, the country would need to maintain a large pool of military personnel so as to rotate forces at regular intervals.

France and the UK fall between the US on the one hand, and Germany on the other. Like the US, both are inclined to participate in offensive operations, but are also more willing than the US to take part in peacekeeping operations. However, for the foreseeable future, France and the UK will lack the capabilities to lead or conduct combat operations like the Kosovo air campaign or the Gulf War without the US, while their long-term global deployments limit the size and duration of their commitments to peace-support operations. France and the UK could build forces capable of playing important roles in *both* combat *and* peace-support operations. As a result, their contributions could be brought to bear in the transition between the combat and peace-support phases of a coalition operation, thereby providing continuity between them. Maintaining strong capabilities and forces for spearheading combat operations will ensure that both London and Paris have a voice in US-led coalitions over the course of a campaign. It will also provide the multinational context that Germany needs if it is to undertake peacekeeping operations. If the UK and France participate in spearhead operations, the US is more likely to do so because the risks and responsibilities would be shared. Professor Colin Gray has argued that, although the full range of US capabilities will remain beyond the means of countries like France and the UK:

> It is not remotely necessary, however, for a close ally to be able to match US military investment, dollar for dollar, for it to be useful, and therefore much respected, in American eyes. Of course, it is preferable to be large and competent. But it is entirely acceptable if one is obliged to settle for being small but still competent.[35]

Harnessing emerging operational concepts and advanced technologies may allow France and the UK to develop 'niche' capabilities – both for combat operations and peace-support missions – that make them indispensable to the Americans and Germans.[36]

However, role specialisation can only be taken so far. A balance must be struck to ensure that political cohesion is maintained in all phases of a coalition operation. This means sharing risks and responsibilities. The US has no interest in being the only country that conducts stand-off precision attacks. Without the participation of other Allies in spearheading a combat operation, the US would lose many of the political benefits of operating in a coalition. On the other hand, the European Allies have no interest in bearing the burdens of peacekeeping without some US involvement. UNPROFOR demonstrated the importance of ensuring that all major members of a coalition participate in a peacekeeping mission. Without risks being shared on the ground, the strategic outlooks of the Allies would quickly diverge. Thus, the participation of some

European Allies in spearheading air and ground-combat operations will be critical, as will some US involvement in the peace-support phase of an operation.]

Conclusion

The US and its European Allies will continue to face threats to their common interests that will necessitate concerted action. While the Allies' preparations were satisfactory during the Cold War for the territorial defence of Europe against the Warsaw Pact, they are inadequate for modern operations. Individually, all the Allies are struggling with the challenges of the modern Western style of warfare: minimising casualties and collateral damage; projecting forces over long distances and into potentially hostile environments with minimal local support; and integrating forces smoothly into complex multinational formations. Collectively, they have failed to ensure sufficient peacetime coordination and multinational planning, and have relied too heavily on *ad hoc* measures in forming and executing coalition responses during crises.

Coalition operations in the 1990s made clear the need for greater peacetime preparations. The European Allies need to develop military capabilities commensurate with Europe's political and economic power. For its part, the US will have to depend more on coalitions if it is to accelerate the rate of change within its own forces to meet longer-term security challenges beyond Europe. Accordingly, both the US and the European Allies must treat multinational action as a central organising principle for defence, and one that affects every facet of their preparations, from equipment acquisition to operational planning and concept development.

The Allies have little choice but to embrace, and adapt their militaries to, the dramatic technological, conceptual and organisational changes that are under way in the military sphere. None of the Allies can contain the effects of an RMA, and all of them face potential risks and opportunities stemming from it. Contrary to the widely held view in Europe, the US probably stands to lose relatively more than its European Allies from these changes, given its current military dominance. Conversely, an RMA may be of relatively greater benefit to the European Allies, given their tighter budgetary constraints. An RMA would enable the Europeans to reduce their force structures and shift to smaller, but more effective, expeditionary forces more rapidly than would have been possible only a few years ago. Moreover, commercially derived technologies and systems are driving down the costs of defence procurement, making equipment more accessible to all, and creating common standards, especially in information systems such as computer operating systems and internet protocols. Finally, the decentralisation of both decision-making and action implies that the European participants in future US-led coalitions will exert more influence over, and have greater insight into, the way in which these operations are planned and run.

NATO will remain an essential framework for defence planning, and for the preparation of forces for coalition operations. Four decades of defence cooperation served the Allies well in the Balkans, and in the Persian Gulf. Nevertheless, preparations based on Cold War experience are increasingly inapplicable. NATO must continue to adapt its doctrine, consultation procedures and operational practices to maintain its relevance as a security framework. Accordingly, it has given greater weight to 'crisis response operations' in its Strategic Concept and has launched the DCI, which will improve the capabilities required to deploy and sustain expeditionary forces, protect them from threats such as missiles and 'cyber attacks', and allow national militaries to operate more effectively together.

Narrowing the discrepancy between the capabilities of the US and those of its European Allies will also require complementary efforts through the EU. If the European Allies are to arrest the slide in their defence budgets and improve their military capabilities for expeditionary operations, the changes must come from within. It is unclear whether the EU's Headline and Capability Goals can be reconciled with the objectives of NATO's DCI. EU members have agreed criteria for sizing their forces which would enable them to play a significant role in future coalitions. However, they have yet to agree criteria for determining the characteristics of those forces, and the capabilities they will require. Whether they focus narrowly on the limited demands of small-scale peacekeeping, or more broadly on the full range of Petersberg tasks, including large-scale combat, will largely determine the direction they take in improving their capacities and their ability to reconcile the EU's initiatives with the Alliance's DCI.

The major Allies must also think beyond the institutional frameworks of NATO and the EU. As the largest and militarily most capable transatlantic Allies, the US, UK, France and Germany should coordinate their defence efforts on a closer, *ad hoc* basis. If they are to achieve a common operational picture in a crisis, they must increase the exchange of intelligence and operational planning in peacetime. Given that future expeditionary operations are likely to be multi-national, planning and doctrine development must also become more multinational. If US operational planning for contingencies outside of Europe is to take greater account of potential European contributions, the European Allies must demonstrate, as the UK already has, that they are willing to participate. Including the Allies in the planning for contingencies in and beyond Europe would make their potential contributions more predictable, and the Allies more reliable coalition partners. Unilateral operational doctrines must become the exception, not the rule; the Allies would, for example, benefit from establishing a centre to develop multinational doctrine.

If forces are to operate outside of Western Europe, their peacetime exercises should focus on cross-regional training. If they are likely to face emerging threats like chemical and biological warfare, missile attacks and terrorism, their exercises should focus on coordinating their defences against these new dangers. NATO has been reluctant both to conduct exercises with a non-European focus, and to incorporate emerging threats into its scenarios. Since the Alliance as a whole is unlikely to engage in operations beyond Europe, the major Allies need to undertake exercises outside of NATO, and to consider integrating their forces outside of established NATO command-and-control hierarchies and procedures. Finally, peacetime consultation between the Allies should increase over rules of engagement and targeting criteria, to ensure that, in future operations, all the parties understand and accept them.

The core transatlantic Allies should also recognise that they need to adopt limited role specialisation based on their political inclinations and comparative military advantages. Dramatic changes in the ways and means by which coalitions are formed, akin to the revolutionary changes under way in military affairs as a whole, are emerging. Coalitions will increasingly be integrated on a temporal basis, as countries agree to participate in specific phases of an operation, rather than signing up to an all-or-nothing proposition. Role specialisation would greatly benefit all of the Allies, and would reduce the need for across-the-board improvements in their capabilities and forces.

Undertaking this kind of peacetime preparation, and taking account of changes in the way that coalitions are formed and managed, would overcome many of the problems revealed by coalition operations in the 1990s. It would also ease political tensions between the Allies, and narrow the differences in their strategic outlooks. Above all, greater individual and collective preparations would help to bring capabilities and concepts into line with the political imperative of concerted military action.

Notes

Acknowledgements

The author would like to thank
Paul Gebhard for his
encouragement and guidance
throughout this project. This paper
benefited from advice and
comments on earlier drafts by
Gordon Adams, Robert Grant,
Andrew Hoehn, Klaus Naumann,
Diego Ruiz Palmer and David Yost.
Above all, the author wishes to
thank his wife Jeanie for her
boundless support and inspiration.

Introduction

[1] This paper defines a coalition
operation as any military action
coordinated and conducted by two
or more countries.
[2] John Chipman, quoted in John D.
Morrocco, 'Kosovo Conflict
Highlights Limits of Airpower and
Capability Gaps', *Aviation Week and
Space Technology*, 17 May 1999,
p. 31.

Chapter 1

[1] UK Ministry of Defence, *Modern
Forces for the Modern World*
(London: The Stationery Office,
1998), para. 77, www.mod.uk.
[2] UK Ministry of Defence,
*Modernising Defence: Annual Report
of Defence Activity 1998/1999*
(London: The Stationery Office,
1999), p. 1, www.mod.uk.
[3] Admiral Sir Michael Boyce, 'The
Commanders Respond', *Proceedings
of the United States Naval Institute*,
vol. 125, no. 1,153, March 1999,
p. 26.
[4] Air Chief Marshal Sir John
Allison, 'The RAF in an Era of
Change', *RUSI Journal*, vol. 144, no.
1, February–March 1999, p. 43.
[5] Michael Codner, 'A Survey of
United Kingdom Military CIS
Programmes', unpublished paper,
Royal United Services Institute
(RUSI), June 1999, p. 8.
[6] Ian Kemp, 'British Army Packs
Double Punch', *Jane's Defence
Weekly*, 28 October 1998, p. 24;
'Interview with General Sir Roger

Wheeler', *ibid.*, 24 February 1999, p. 32.

[7] 'Financial and Economic Data Relating to NATO Defence', *NATO Press Release M-DPC-2(98)147*, 17 December 1998, p. 3, www.nato.int.

[8] Michael Evans, 'Robertson Cuts Swath Through the TA', *The Times*, 18 November 1998, p. 1.

[9] Michael J. Witt, 'British Call Off Deal for Airlift', *Defense News*, vol. 14, no. 32, 16 August 1999, pp. 3, 20.

[10] Ministry of Defence, *Defence White Paper 1999* (London: Ministry of Defence, 1999), chap. 3, para. 40, www.mod.uk.

[11] John Ross, 'Overstretch in UK Armed Forces', *RUSI Newsbrief*, August 1999, vol. 19, no. 8, p. 59.

[12] IISS, *The Military Balance, 1999/ 2000* (Oxford: Oxford University Press for the IISS, 1999), p. 78. Of this total of 41,788, 20,800 are stationed in Germany alone. Most of these would be available for deployments in coalition operations. At the peak in 1999, over 14,000 British troops were in the Balkans, and in Italy as part of the Stabilisation Force (SFOR)'s air component. By mid-2000, the UK's Balkan presence had fallen to around 7,000.

[13] IISS, *The Military Balance 1999/ 2000*, pp. 75, 77.

[14] Press Conference by the Secretary of State for Defence, The Rt. Hon. Geoffrey Hoon MP, Ministry of Defence, London, 20 December 1999, www.mod.uk.

[15] Ministry of Defence, *Defence White Paper 1999*, chap. 4, para. 70; Press Conference by the Secretary of State for Defence, 20 December 1999.

[16] Ministry of Defence, *Defence White Paper 1999*, chap. 4, para. 70.

[17] Philip Sherwell, David Cracknell and David Wastell, 'Blair Pledges 50,000 for Invasion', *Sunday Telegraph*, 30 May 1999, p. 1.

[18] Ross, 'Overstretch'.

[19] See Michael Evans, 'Army Chiefs Say Kosovo Guns Were Unreliable', *The Times*, 4 January 2000, pp. 1, 4.

[20] Interview with Vice-Admiral Ian Garnett by Rear-Admiral (retired) Richard Cobbold, 'My Job: The Challenge of Joint Command', *RUSI Journal*, vol. 144, no. 4, August 1999, p. 8.

[21] Diego Ruiz Palmer, 'France's Military Command Structures in the 1990s', in Thomas-Durell Young (ed.), *Command in NATO after the Cold War: Alliance, National, and Multinational Considerations* (Carlyle Barracks, PA: Strategic Studies Institute, 1997), p. 100.

[22] Peter C. Hunt, *Coalition Warfare: Considerations for the Air Component Commander* (Maxwell Air Force Base, AL: Air University Press, 1998), p. 29.

[23] Thomas Keaney and Eliot A. Cohen, *Gulf War Air Power Survey Summary Report* (Washington DC: US Government Printing Office (USGPO), 1993), p. 220.

[24] Pierre Joxe, speech to the National Assembly, 6 June 1991, quoted in David S. Yost, 'France and the Revolution in Military Affairs', unpublished paper, 31 March 1997, p. 16.

[25] Ministère de la Defense, *Livre Blanc sur la Defense* (Paris: Service d'Information et de Relations Publiques des Armées, February 1994), p. i.

[26] *Ibid.*, pp. 46–47.

[27] Ministère de la Defense, *Livre Blanc sur la Defense* (Paris: Ministère de la Defense, 1972); also see Philip H. Gordon, *A Certain Idea of France: French Security Policy and the Gaullist Legacy* (Princeton, NJ: Princeton University Press, 1993), pp. 70–71.

[28] Ministère de la Defense, *Premiers Enseignements des Opérations au Kosovo: Analyses et Références* (Paris: Ministère de la Defense, June 1999), p. 13.

[29] Ruiz Palmer, 'France's Military Command Structures in the 1990s', pp. 104–105.

[30] Patrice-Henry Desaubliaux, *Le Figaro*, 3 March 1997, p. 7.

[31] Jacques Isnard, 'La France s'Engage à Déployer jusqu'à 50,000 Hommes pour l'Alliance Atlantique', *Le Monde*, 2 July 1998, p. 32.

[32] Jean-Dominique Merchet, *Libération*, 29 April 1999, p. 13.

[33] Phillip J. Gick, 'NATO's Force Projection: Where's the Lift?', unpublished paper, June 1998.

[34] Telephone interview with NATO official, April 2000; speech by Defence Minister Alain Richard at the Military Academy, Paris, 9 April 1998, www.defense.gouv.fr; also see Jean-Marc Tanguy, 'France's Programme Review', *Military Technology*, June 1998, pp. 98–101.

[35] J. A. C. Lewis, 'France Slashes Military Budget by $1.45 bn', *Jane's Defence Weekly*, 1 December 1999, p. 3.

[36] Ministère de la Defense, *Budget de la Defense 1999*, www.defense.gouv.fr.

[37] Germany contributes forces to six multinational corps formations, more than any other Ally: the Allied Command Europe Rapid Reaction Corps (ARRC), the Eurocorps, the First German–Dutch Corps, the Second and Fifth German–US Corps and the Multinational Corps Northeast, with Denmark and Poland. Germany also contributes forces to the air-mobile NATO Multinational Division – Central, the Allied Command Europe (ACE) Mobile Force – Land, and the Franco-German Brigade.

[38] Bundesministerium der Verteidigung, *Weißbuch 1994 zur Sicherheit der Bundesrepublik Deutschland und zur Lage und Zukunft der Bundeswehr* (Bonn: Bundesministerium der Verteidigung, 1994), p. 41.

[39] Bundesministerium der Verteidigung, *Bestandaufnahme: Die Bundeswehr an der Schwelle zum 21. Jahrhundert* (Bonn: Bundesministerium der Verteidigung, 1999), p. 52.

[40] *Ibid.*, p. 66.

[41] *Ibid.*, p. 75.

[42] Ronald D. Asmus, *Germany's Contribution to Peacekeeping: Issues and Outlook* (Santa Monica, CA: RAND, 1995), p. 3.

[43] 'Germany and Kosovo', *The Economist*, 24 April 1999, p. 49.

[44] Bundesministerium der Verteidigung, *Bestandaufnahme*, p. 130.

[45] *Ibid.*, pp. 20–21.

[46] Karl Feldmeyer, 'Eine Neue Ratlosigkeit', *Frankfurter Allgemeine Zeitung*, 25 June 1999, p. 1.

[47] Bundesministerium der Verteidigung, *Bestandaufnahme*, p. 130.

[48] 'Financial and Economic Data Relating to NATO Defence', p. 7.

[49] Heinz Schulte, 'Country Briefing: Germany', *Jane's Defence Weekly*, 7 July 1999, p. 26.

[50] *Streitkräfteeinsatz 2020* (Bonn: Bundeswehr Amt für Studien und Übungen, 1996), pp. 17–18.

[51] Rolf Portz, 'The Luftwaffe on the Way to the 21st Century', *Military Technology*, Special Issue, 1998, p. 40.

[52] Karl Schwarz, 'Conceptual Realignment Is Unavoidable', *Flug Revue*, August 1999, pp. 64–66, in Foreign Broadcast Information Service (FBIS), *Daily Report*, FBIS-

WEU-1999-0803, 1 August 1999.

[53] Schulte, 'Country Briefing'.

[54] Alexander Szandar, 'Schnupperkurs beim Bund', *Der Spiegel*, 18 January 1999, pp. 64–65.

[55] Franz-Josef Meiers, 'A German Defense Review?', paper presented at the seminar on 'European Force Structures', Western European Union (WEU) Institute for Security Studies, Paris, 27–28 May 1999, p. 1.

[56] Interviews with German defence officials, Bonn, August 1999.

[57] Szandar, 'Schnupperkurs beim Bund'.

[58] Interview with Defence Minister Rudolf Scharping by Tilman Gerwein and Michael Stoessinger, 'Ja, es gibt Schwachstellen', *Stern*, 11 March 1999, pp. 228–31.

[59] Schulte, 'Country Briefing'.

[60] William S. Cohen, *Report of the Quadrennial Defense Review* (Washington DC: Department of Defense, 1997), pp. 8, 11.

[61] *Ibid.*

[62] Colin Clark, 'US Offers to Extend Experimentation Process to Allies', *Defense News*, 16–22 November 1998, p. 6.

[63] Ted Gold, 'Task Force on Coalition Warfare: Draft Final Report', unpublished briefing by the Defense Science Board, Washington DC, March 1999.

[64] David C. Gompert and Richard L. Kugler, *Rebuilding the Team: How to Get Allies To Do More in Defense of Common Interests* (Santa Monica, CA: RAND, 1996), p. 1.

[65] John E. Reilly, *American Public Opinion and US Foreign Policy 1999* (Chicago, IL: Chicago Council on Foreign Relations, 1999), p. 16.

[66] National Defense Panel, *Transforming Defense: National Security in the Twenty-first Century* (Washington DC: US Department of Defense, 1997), pp. 57–59.

[67] See Dan Gouré and Jeffrey M. Ranney, *Averting the Defense Trainwreck in the New Millennium* (Washington DC: Center for Strategic and International Studies (CSIS), 1999), p. 2.

[68] See Steve Kosiak, *CSIS Train Wreck Analysis Is Off Track*, (Washington DC: Center for Strategic and Budgetary Assessments, 7 February 2000), www.csbaonline.org.

[69] Eliot A. Cohen, 'What To Do about National Defense', *Commentary*, November 1994, p. 25.

Chapter 2

[1] US Department of Defense, *Conduct of the Persian Gulf War: Final Report to Congress* (Washington DC: Department of Defense, 1992), p. xxvii.

[2] George Bush and Brent Scowcroft, *A World Transformed* (New York: Alfred A. Knopf, 1998), pp. 448–49.

[3] Keaney and Cohen, *Gulf War Air Power Survey Summary Report*, p. 158. Saudi officers also joined the staff of the 'Black Hole', but no French military officers were included.

[4] Hunt, *Coalition Warfare*, p. 26.

[5] Bruce George and Joe Sanderson, 'Financial and Non-Military Support for the Coalition', in Bruce L. Watson (ed.), *Military Lessons of the Gulf War* (London: Greenhill Books, 1991), Appendix A, p. 221; Rod Alonso and Bruce W. Watson, 'Air Forces', in *ibid.*, Appendix D, pp. 226–27; and Peter Tsouras, Elmo C. Wright Jr. and Bruce W. Watson, 'Ground Forces', in *ibid.*, Appendix E, pp. 240–41. The US provided 1,376 combat aircraft and 532,000 ground troops; the UK 69 combat aircraft and approximately 35,000 troops; and France 42

combat aircraft and approximately 13,500 troops. Germany contributed $8.9 billion, as well as over $2bn in aid to Egypt, Jordan, Turkey and Israel. Germany also provided field medical facilities and road, rail, air and sea transport for Allied forces moving from Germany to the Gulf.

6 Even French armed forces, which did not formally participate in the Alliance's integrated military structure, had a basic understanding of the manoeuvre style of warfare embodied in NATO doctrine, although French national military doctrine remained distinct.

7 Stephen J. Flanagan, *NATO's Conventional Defences* (London: Macmillan, 1988), pp. 87–90.

8 William G. Pagonis with Jeffrey Cruikshank, *Moving Mountains: Lessons in Leadership and Logistics from the Gulf War* (Boston, MA: Harvard Business School Press, 1992), pp. 75–76.

9 Interview with Group Captain Andrew Lambert, Incirlik, Turkey, August 1999.

10 Quoted in David S. Yost, 'France and the Gulf War of 1990–1991: Political–Military Lessons Learned', *Journal of Strategic Studies*, vol. 16, no. 3, September 1993, p. 355.

11 IISS, *The Military Balance 1990–1991* (London: Brassey's for the IISS, 1990), pp. 66, 85.

12 *Ibid.*, pp. 23–24, 66, 68, 85.

13 *Conduct of the Persian Gulf War*, p. 590.

14 Hunt, *Coalition Warfare*, p. 32.

15 Speech by Rt. Hon. George Robertson, RUSI conference on NATO, London, March 1999.

16 Gilles Andréani, 'France and the Alliance after the Cold War', *RUSI Journal*, vol. 144, no. 1, February–March 1999, p. 22.

17 Interview with Colonel P. R. Wilkinson, Royal Army Directorate of Doctrine Development, London, January 1999.

18 *Joint Doctrine for Military Operations Other Than War*, US Joint Pub 3-07 (Washington DC: Department of Defense, 1995).

19 Peter D. Feaver and Christopher Gelpi, 'How Many Deaths Are Acceptable? A Surprising Answer', *Washington Post*, 7 November 1999, p. B3.

20 Bernard de Bressy, 'La Guerre "Zéro Mort" un Rêve Americain?', *Defense Nationale*, no. 55, April 1999, pp. 22–29.

21 *Peace Support Operations*, Joint Warfare Publication 3-50 (Northwood: Permanent Joint Headquarters, 1998), pp. 4–11.

22 Interview with Colonel Phil Wilkinson, Royal Army Directorate of Doctrine Development, London, January 1999.

23 Colonel P. R. Wilkinson, 'Sharpening the Weapons of Peace', *British Army Review*, no. 118, April 1998, p. 4.

24 Roger H. Palin, *Multinational Military Forces: Problems and Prospects*, Adelphi Paper 294 (Oxford: Oxford University Press for the IISS, 1995), p. 47.

25 Many of the Allied contributions comprised less than 1,000 personnel: Belgium (300), Denmark (800), Greece (1,000), Luxembourg (300), Norway (750) and Portugal (900). Non-NATO contributions tended to be even smaller, including: Austria (300), Latvia (40), Lithuania (40), Slovakia (406) and Ukraine (500). See US Department of Defense Scientific and Technical Information Program, *Operation Joint Endeavor Fact Sheet 006-B*, 11 December 1995, www.dtic.mil/bosnia/fs/fs006b.html.

26 Barbara Starr, 'Learning Zone: SFOR's Experience in Bosnia', *Jane's Defence Weekly*, 27 May 1998, p. 24.

27 Interview with General Klaus Naumann, Munich, August 1999.

28 Larry K. Wentz, 'C4ISR Systems and Services', in Larry K. Wentz (ed.), *Lessons From Bosnia: The IFOR Experience* (Washington DC: National Defense University (NDU), 1997), pp. 351, 359.

29 *Ibid.*, p. 359.

30 *Ibid.*, p. 375.

31 *Ibid.*, p. 53.

32 Eric Schmitt, 'Germany's Leader Pledges to Block Combat on Ground', *New York Times*, 20 May 1999, p. 1.

33 Prepared testimony of General Wesley K. Clark before the US Senate Armed Services Committee, 21 October 1999.

34 Ministère de la Defense, *Les Enseignements du Kosovo: Analyses et Références* (Paris: Ministère de la Defense, November 1999), p. 9.

35 Deputy Secretary of State Strobe Talbott, 'America's Stake in a Strong Europe', remarks at a conference on the future of NATO, RUSI, London, 7 October 1999, www.state.gov.

36 US Department of Defense, *Report to Congress: Kosovo/Operation Allied Force After-Action Report* (Washington DC: US Department of Defense, 31 January 2000), pp. 47–48.

37 Steven Lee Myers, 'Chinese Embassy Bombing: A Wide Net of Blame', *New York Times*, 17 April 2000, p. 1.

38 Interviews with senior military officers at Allied Forces Southern Europe (AFSOUTH) Headquarters, Naples, July 1999, and with Allied staff at the Combined Air Operations Centre (CAOC), Vicenza, August 1999.

39 Interview with Lieutenant-General Michael Short, Allied Air Forces Southern Europe (AIRSOUTH) Headquarters, Naples, July 1999.

40 Craig Whitney, 'US Military Acted Outside NATO Framework During Kosovo Conflict, France Says', *New York Times*, 11 November 1999, p. 1.

41 US Department of Defense, *Report to Congress: Kosovo*, p. 45.

42 Interview with Lieutenant-General Short, July 1999.

43 Myers, 'Chinese Embassy Bombing'; and Ministère de la Defense, *Les Enseignements du Kosovo*, p. 10.

44 Interview with President Jacques Chirac by Elise Lucet *et al.*, Palais de L'Elysée, Paris, 14 July 1999, www.elysee.fr.

45 Richard Parker, 'Bombing Alone Can't Stop Milosevic, NATO Generals Say', *Miami Herald*, 22 May 1999, www.herald.com.

46 Neil King, 'General Warns NATO to Expect More Bombing, Civilian Casualties', *Wall Street Journal*, 27 May 1999, p. 21.

47 Press conference by General Wesley K. Clark, 16 September 1999, www.nato.int.

48 Interviews with Allied air planners, CAOC, August 1999.

49 Roger Cohen, 'In a Breach, German Party Backs "Limited Halt" in Kosovo Air War', *New York Times*, 14 May 1999, p. 1; and George Jones and Ben Fenton, 'Blair Paves Way for Ground Troops', *Daily Telegraph*, 22 April 1999, p. 1.

50 David A. Deptula, *Firing for Effect: Change in the Nature of Warfare*, Defense and Airpower Series (Arlington, VA: Aerospace Education Association, 1995), p. 6.

51 Harlan K. Ullman, James P. Wade *et al.*, *Shock and Awe: Achieving Rapid Dominance* (Washington DC:

USGPO, 1996), p. 12.

52 Jean-Jacques Mevel, *Le Figaro*, 20 April 1999, p. 5.

53 Ministère de la Defense, *Les Enseignements du Kosovo*, p. 19.

54 Secretary of Defense William S. Cohen and Chairman of the Joint Chiefs of Staff General Henry Shelton, Joint Statement on the Kosovo After Action Review before the Senate Armed Services Committee, 14 October 1999, www.defenselink.mil.

55 Carla Anne Robbins, 'Display of US Might Makes Allies, Adversaries Doubt Their Relevance', *Wall Street Journal*, 6 July 1999, p. 1.

56 Ministère de la Defense, *Premiers Enseignements des Opérations au Kosovo*, p. 7; British Ministry of Defence, *Kosovo: An Account of the Crisis* (London: Ministry of Defence, 1999), www.mod.uk.

57 Ministère de la Defense, *Premiers Enseignements des Opérations au Kosovo*, p. 7.

58 Interview with senior Allied officials, AFSOUTH Headquarters, Naples, July 1999.

59 Robert Wall, 'Airspace Control Challenges Allies', *Aviation Week and Space Technology*, 26 April 1999, p. 30.

60 David A. Fulghum, 'NATO Unprepared for Electronic Combat', *ibid.*, 10 May 1999, p. 35.

61 Greg Siegle, 'Radar-Jamming Prowlers Played Big Role in the Balkans', *Jane's Defence Weekly*, 7 July 1999.

62 Morrocco, 'Kosovo Conflict Highlights Limits of Airpower and Capability Gaps', p. 31; interview with Allied planners, CAOC, August 1999.

63 Leighton W. Smith, *NATO's IFOR in Action: Lessons from the Bosnian Peace Support Operations*, Strategic Forum 154 (Washington DC: NDU,

1999), p. 2.

64 British Ministry of Defence, *Kosovo: An Account of the Crisis*.

65 Interview with Allied intelligence officers, AFSOUTH Headquarters, July 1999.

66 Andrew Gilligan, 'RAF Admits Failings in Kosovo Inquiry', *Sunday Telegraph*, 25 July 1999, p. 8.

67 Rowan Scarborough, 'Kosovo Target Data Stalled in Transit', *Washington Times*, 28 July 1999, p. A11.

68 Interviews with senior Allied military officers, CAOC, August 1999; Vago Muradian, 'Kosovo Will Be to Post-2000 as Gulf War Was to 1990s', *Defense Daily*, 27 April 1999, p. 7.

69 Douglas Barrie, 'Britain Examines UAV as Surrogate Satellite', *Defense News*, 17 May 1999, p. 4; interview with Colonel Karl-Heinz Drechsler of the German Ministry of Defence, Paris, June 1999.

70 Interview with French Defence Minister Alain Richard by Jean-Gabriel Fredet, *Le Nouvel Observateur*, 15 July 1999.

71 Ministère de la Defense, *Premiers Enseignements des Opérations au Kosovo*, p. 5.

72 *Ibid.*

73 Linda D. Kozaryn, 'Cohen Calls on Allies to Share the Load', *American Forces Press Service*, 8 July 1999, www.defenselink.mil/briefings.

74 Interview with communications officers, AFSOUTH Headquarters, July 1999.

75 US Department of Defense, *Report to Congress: Kosovo/Operation Allied Force After-Action Report*, p. 74.

76 *Ibid.*, pp. 47–48.

77 *Ibid.*, p. 49.

78 Bryan Bender, 'Allies Still Lack Real-Time Targeting', *Jane's Defence*

Weekly, 7 April 1999, p. 4.
[79] Interviews with operations officers, CAOC, August 1999; Dana Priest, 'Serbs Listening In on Pilots', *Washington Post*, 1 May 1999, p. A1; David A. Fulghum and Robert Wall, 'Data Link, EW Problems Pinpointed by Pentagon', *Aviation Week and Space Technology*, 6 September 1999, p. 87.
[80] Admiral James O. Ellis, 'A View from the Top', unpublished presentation on Joint Task Force *Noble Anvil*, August 1999.
[81] Muradian, 'Kosovo Will Be to Post-2000 As Gulf War Was to 1990s', p. 7.
[82] Ministère de la Defense, *Les Enseignements du Kosovo*, p. 19.
[83] Fulghum and Wall, 'Weapons, Intelligence Targeted in Probe', *Aviation Week and Space Technology*, 26 July 1999, p. 71.
[84] Ministère de la Defense, *Premiers Enseignements des Opérations au Kosovo*, p. 6.
[85] Michael Evans, 'Review of RAF's Weapons Systems', *The Times*, 8 July 1999, p. 15.
[86] Schulte, 'Country Briefing: Germany', p. 32.
[87] Jean-Dominique Merchet, *Libération*, 29 April 1999, p. 13.

Chapter 3

[1] See Earl H. Tilford, *The Revolution in Military Affairs: Prospects and Cautions* (Carlisle Barracks, PA: US Army War College Strategic Studies Institute, 1995), p. 1.
[2] William A. Owens, 'The Emerging System of Systems', *Proceedings of the United States Naval Institute*, vol. 121, no. 1,107, May 1995, pp. 36–39.
[3] Klaus Naumann, 'An Overview of Alliance Military Issues', speech to the North Atlantic Assembly Plenary Session, Barcelona, 26 May 1998, www.nato.int.
[4] UK Ministry of Defence, *Modern Forces for the Modern World* (London: The Stationery Office, 1998), para. 33; Speech by French Defence Minister Richard at the Institut des Hautes Etudes de Defense Nationale (IHEDN), Paris, 10 February 1998, www.defense.gouv.fr; Cohen, *Report of the Quadrennial Defense Review*, pp. 13–14; *Streitkräfteeinsatz 2020*, vol. 1, p. 12.
[5] Alexander Nicoll, 'Sea Lord Warns on Military Technology Gap', *Financial Times*, 7 October 1998, p. 8. Other analysts have voiced similar concerns. See, for example, Gerrard Quille, 'The Revolution in Military Affairs and the UK', *International Security Information Service Briefing 73*, December 1998; Lawrence Freedman, 'War Designed for One', *The World Today*, vol. 53, nos 8–9, August–September 1997, pp. 217–22; Yves Boyer, 'This Way to the Revolution', *RUSI Journal*, vol. 14, no. 2, April–May 1999, pp. 46–48; and Yost, 'France and the Revolution in Military Affairs'.
[6] Robbin F. Laird and Holger H. Mey, *The Revolution in Military Affairs: Allied Perspectives*, McNair Paper 60 (Washington DC: NDU, 1999), p. 80.
[7] US Commission on National Security, *New World Coming: American Security in the Twenty-first Century*, Phase 1 Report (Washington DC: Department of Defense, 15 September 1999), pp. 64, 143.
[8] Andrew F. Krepinevich, *Transforming America's Alliances* (Washington DC: Center for Strategic and Budgetary Assessments, February 2000), p. ii.
[9] Pierre Fiorini, *CORI: Conséquences Opérationnelles de la Révolution de*

l'Information (Paris: Centre de Recherches et d'Etudes sur les Stratégies et les Technologies (CREST), May 1998), p. 101.

[10] Yves Boyer, 'National Perspectives on Coalition Interoperability', unpublished paper presented to the RUSI Conference on 'The Implications of Technological Innovation for Coalition Operations/ Interoperability', London, 25–26 February 1999, p. 5; Fiorini, *CORI,* p. 101.

[11] Richard E. Hayes, *Linking Current and Future Coalition C4ISR,* unpublished paper, 6 October 1999, www.uscrest.org.

[12] Martha Mauer, *Coalition Command and Control* (Washington DC: NDU, 1994), pp. 117–99.

[13] Freedman, 'War Designed for One'.

[14] This view has gained currency in, for example, the British Ministry of Defence. Interview with Captain Simon Branch-Evans, British Ministry of Defence, London, December 1998.

[15] Michael G. Vickers and Robert C. Martinage, *The Military Revolution and Intrastate Conflict* (Washington DC: Center for Strategic and Budgetary Assessments, October 1997), p. 32.

[16] *Ibid.*

[17] Michael J. Mazarr, *The Revolution in Military Affairs: A Framework for Defense Planning* (Carlisle Barracks, PA: US Army War College Strategic Studies Institute, 1994), p. 26.

[18] Chairman of the Joint Chiefs of Staff, *Joint Vision 2010* (Washington DC: US Department of Defense, 1996). *Joint Vision* assumes that US military forces will have an advantage over any opponent in terms of information about the battle area, including knowledge of the strength and location of both friendly and opposing forces. This will provide greater opportunities for manoeuvre, precision attacks, leaner logistics and greater force protection.

[19] *Ibid.*, p. 9.

[20] Richard Haass, *The Reluctant Sheriff: The United States after the Cold War* (New York: Brookings Institution Press, 1997), p. 98.

[21] NATO did this in the 1991 Gulf War, when it endorsed politically the actions of its members which contributed forces to the multinational coalition. During the Gulf conflict, the Alliance also increased the defences of a front-line state, Turkey, and stepped up its naval presence in the Mediterranean.

[22] The Alliance's Strategic Concept, approved by Heads of State and Government participating in the meeting of the North Atlantic Council in Washington DC, 24 April 1999, www.nato.int.

[23] Washington Summit Communiqué issued by the Heads of State and Government participating in the meeting of the North Atlantic Council, Washington DC, 24 April 1999, www.nato.int.

[24] Harold W. Gehman, 'Transforming NATO Defense Capabilities', *Joint Force Quarterly,* no. 21, Spring 1999, p. 50.

[25] Nicholas de Chezelles, 'The NATO Agenda and International Interoperability', paper presented to the RUSI Conference on 'The Implications of Technological Innovation for Coalition Operations/Interoperability', p. 6.

[26] George Robertson, quoted in Roger Cohen, 'Dependent on US Now, Europe Vows Defense Push', *New York Times,* 12 May 1999, p. A12.

[27] President of the European Union,

~~Conclusions~~, Helsinki, 10–11
December 1999, www.europa.int.
[28] See Western European Union
Council of Ministers, *Petersberg
Declaration*, Bonn, Germany, 19
June 1992, www.weu.int.
[29] Bryan Bender, 'Exercise Heralds
Cross-Regional Training for
NATO', *Jane's Defence Weekly*, 3
November 1999, p. 2.
[30] David C. Gompert, Richard L.
Kugler and Martin C. Libicki, *Mind
the Gap: Promoting a Transatlantic
Revolution in Military Affairs*
(Washington DC: NDU Press,
1999), p. 15.
[31] Lawrence Freedman, *The
Revolution in Strategic Affairs*,
Adelphi Paper 318 (Oxford: Oxford
University Press for the IISS, 1998).
[32] Quille, *The Revolution in Military
Affairs and the UK*.
[33] Interview with Captain Simon
Branch-Evans, London, December
1998.
[34] 'Peacekeeping Undermines US
Combat Readiness', *Jane's Defence
Weekly*, 28 July 1999.
[35] Colin S. Gray, *The American
Revolution in Military Affairs: An
Interim Assessment*, Occasional
Paper 28 (Camberley: Strategic and
Combat Studies Institute, 1997),
p. 52.
[36] Herbert Kremp, 'Amerika,
Europa und die Moderne Kunst
des Krieges', *Die Welt*, 16 February
1998.